JESUS, OUR MAN IN GLORY

A·W·TOZER

JESUS, OUR MAN IN GLORY

COMPILED AND EDITED BY

GERALD B. SMITH

CHRISTIAN PUBLICATIONS

Camp Hill, Pennsylvania

Christian Publications
3825 Hartzdale Drive, Camp Hill, PA 17011

The mark of ✝ *vibrant faith*

ISBN: 0-87509-390-6
LOC Catalog Card Number: 87-70163
© 1987 by Christian Publications
All rights reserved
Printed in the United States of America

Cover photo: "Ascension of Christ" by Tiffany Studios, circa 1902. Grace United Methodist Church, Harrisburg, PA. Photo by Mike Saunier.

First printing of trade paper edition 1987

95 96 97 98 99   6 5 4 3 2

CONTENTS

INTRODUCTION

THOSE WHO HEARD A.W. TOZER only at the popular, mid-20th century Bible conferences considered him a topical preacher who dealt mainly with the striking Bible texts.

His congregations in Chicago and Toronto knew better! They treasured his pastoral preaching from Sunday to Sunday, month by month, year after year. His sermons were a thorough-going, depth-charged examination and exploration of the Scriptures as the revealed and inspired Word of God.

While in his long pastorate in Chicago, Dr. Tozer felt that he was "comfortably started" in the consideration of the Gospel of John after he had been preaching from the book for more than two years! In Toronto, too, his congregation soon discovered that their pastor's insistent and incisive preaching was his own method of potent Bible teaching.

Not long before his death in 1963, Tozer completed a Sunday morning series of 40 sermons from the book of Hebrews. When he began the series, he made it plain to his listeners that the eternal glories of Jesus Christ, the Son of God, would glow forth in every message. He also said he took exception to the remark of a ministerial friend that "most people find the book of Hebrews pretty dull material."

The 12 chapters of this book, to be followed in due course by a companion volume completing Tozer's exposition of Hebrews, are a record of his findings. Clearly, he was right. The person and glory of Jesus Christ shine forth through every part of this inspired letter to the Hebrews.

Gerald B. Smith

CHAPTER

1

Jesus, Our Man in Glory

HAVE YOU HEARD any sermons lately on the Bible truth that our risen Savior and Lord is now our glorified Man and Mediator? That He is seated at the right hand of the Majesty in the heavenlies?

Few Christians are fully aware of Christ's high-priestly office at the throne. I suspect this is a neglected subject in evangelical preaching and teaching. It is a major theme in the letter to the Hebrews. The teaching is plain: Jesus is there, risen and glorified, at the right hand of the Majesty on high, representing the believing children of God, His church on earth.

Here is one of the great Biblical encouragements to acknowledge Jesus and to trust Him in His priestly ministry for us:

> Since we have a great high priest who has gone through the heavens, Jesus the Son of God, let us hold firmly to the faith we profess. For we do not have a high priest who is unable to sympathize with our weaknesses, but we have one who has been tempted in every way, just as we are—yet was without sin. Let us then approach the throne of grace with confidence, so that we may receive mercy and find grace to help us in our time of need. (Hebrews 4:14–16)

3

The Scriptures assure us that there is a true tabernacle—a true sanctuary in heaven. Jesus our great High Priest is busy there. In that heavenly sanctuary is a continuing and effective altar. There is a mercy seat. Best of all, our Mediator and Advocate is there on our behalf. What an amazing truth!

Amazing—and yet how difficult it seems for us to comprehend it and to count on it. In the light of God's gracious revelation, I can only ask in humility and chagrin, "Why are we so ineffective in representing Him? Why are we so apathetic in living for Him and glorifying Him?"

Everything about Jesus is glorious

It is well for us to confess often that everything the Father has revealed concerning Jesus Christ is glorious. His past—as we would humanly look on the past—is glorious, for He made all things that were made. His work on earth as the Son of Man was glorious, for He effected the plan of salvation through His death and resurrection. Then He ascended into the heavenlies for His mediatorial ministries throughout this present age.

In view of what the Scriptures tell us of Jesus, it should be our primary concern to show forth the eternal glories of this One who is our divine Savior and Lord.

In our world are dozens of different kinds of Christianities. Certainly many of them do not seem to be busy and joyful in proclaiming the unique glories of Jesus Christ as the eternal Son of God. Some brands of Christianity will tell you very quickly that they are just trying to do a little bit of good on behalf of neglected people and neglected causes. Others will affirm that we can do more good by joining in the "contemporary dialogue" than by continuing to proclaim the "old, old story of the cross."

But we stand with the early Christian apostles. We believe that every Christian proclamation should be to the glory and the praise of the One whom God raised up after He had loosed the pains of death. I am happy to be identified with Peter and his message at Pentecost:

> Jesus of Nazareth was a man accredited by God to you by miracles, wonders and signs, which God did among you through him, as you yourselves know. This man was handed over to you by God's set purpose and foreknowledge; and you, with the help of wicked men, put him to death by nailing him to the cross. But God raised him from the dead, freeing him from the agony of death, because it was impossible for death to keep its hold on him. (Acts 2:22–24)

Peter considered it important to affirm that the risen Christ is now exalted at the right hand of God. He said that fact was the reason for the coming of the Holy Spirit. Frankly, I am too busy serving Jesus to spend my time and energy engaging in contemporary dialogue.

We have a commission from heaven

I think I know what "contemporary dialogue" means. It means that all of those intellectual preachers are busy reading the news magazines so they will be able to comment on the world situation from their pulpits on Sunday mornings. But that is not what God called me to do. He called me to preach the glories of Christ. He commissioned me to tell my people there is a kingdom of God and a throne in the heavens. And that we have One of our own representing us there.

That is what the early church was excited about. And I think our Lord may have reason to ask why we are no longer very excited about it. The Christian church in the first century was ablaze with this concept of the risen and victorious Christ exalted at the right hand of the Father. Although it worshiped no other man, it urged the worship of this glorified and exalted Man as God, because He had always been the eternal Son, the second Person of the Godhead. Paul wrote to Timothy:

> There is one God and one mediator between God and men, the man Christ Jesus, who gave himself as a ransom for all men—the testimony given in its proper time. (1 Timothy 2:5–6)

Consider with me some of the things we know about the priesthood for which God anointed our Lord Jesus. Not only was He the eternal Son, but He was also the glorified Man. Why should we ignore the reality of such a priesthood and treat it as if it was some appendage to religious forms and traditions?

Priesthood in the Old Testament

The true idea of the priesthood, as it was developed in the Old Testament and fulfilled by our Lord Jesus Christ, was ordained by God. It came from His mind and heart. It was dimly foreshadowed in the lives of praying fathers, heads of their households, who assumed responsibility and concern for their families.

Job was a good example of this kind of Old Testament family priest. Afraid his children might have sinned, he prayed to God, asking Him to forgive and cleanse them. But the concept is much more clearly embodied in the Levitical priesthood, ordained by God for Israel's forgiveness and cleansing. In its final perfection, the priesthood is portrayed in Jesus Christ, our Lord.

We must acknowledge that God's concept of the priesthood arose from man's alienation from God. It is based on the fact that man has strayed from God and is lost. This is a fundamental part of truth, just as surely as hydrogen is a part of water. You cannot have water without hydrogen. Just as surely, you cannot have Bible truth without the teaching that mankind has broken with God and fallen from his first created estate, where he was made in God's image.

God's concept and instructions are very plain. There has been a moral breach. Sinning man has violated the laws of God. In other words, man is a moral criminal before the bar of God. It is clear from the Bible that a sinful man or woman cannot return to God's favor and fellowship until justice is satisfied, until the breach is healed.

In an effort to heal the breach, man has used many subtleties and rationalizations. But if he rejects the cross of Christ, if he rejects God's plan of salvation, if he rejects Christ's death and resurrection as the basis for atonement, there is no remaining ground for redemption. Reconciliation is an impossibility.

It is a part of my calling and responsibility in the ministry to warn men and women that rejection of the atoning work of Jesus Christ is fatal to the soul. With such rejection, the efforts of the Savior and His intercession as great High Priest have no meaning.

Man is at fault

Alienation was not God's fault. It was man who alienated himself. Man is away from God, like a little island that has pulled away from the mainland. Drifting out to sea, it has lost the attraction of its original position. So man has morally pulled away from God and from the attraction of God's fellowship. Man is alienated, without hope and without God in this world.

The important element in God's concept of the priesthood is mediatorship. The Old Testament priest provided a means of reconciliation between God and man. But he had to be ordained of God. Otherwise, he was a false priest. In order to help man, he had to be appointed by God.

God, for His part, needs no help. There never was an Old Testament priest who could help God. The work of the priest was to offer a sacrifice, an atonement, so that alienated man could be forgiven and cleansed. In the Levitical order, an offering had to be made to God by the priest on behalf of the sinner. The priest was appointed to plead the case of man before a righteous God.

That ancient priestly system was not perfect. It was only the shadow of a perfect, eternal priesthood to be brought about by the Savior-Priest, Jesus Christ, the eternal Son. Every priest in the order of Levi knew only too well his own sin. This was the point of the breakdown. When that priest stood before God in the holiest place to present an atonement for the sins of the people, he was face-to-face as well with the reality of his own failures and shortcomings.

In our own day, we recognize what this means to us as liberated and forgiven believers. Singing the hymnody of Isaac Watts, we revel in Christ's atonement and God's forgiveness:

Not all the blood of beasts
    On Jewish altars slain,
Could give the guilty conscience peace,
    Or wash away the stain.

But Christ, the heavenly Lamb,
    Takes all our sins away;
A sacrifice of nobler name,
    And richer blood than they.

The Old Testament priest knew that the ritual of sacrifice could not completely atone for sins or change man's sinful nature. In that priestly system, God "covered" the sin until the time when Christ would come. Christ, the Lamb of God, would completely bear away the sin of the world.

Jesus our Lord qualified completely to be our great High Priest. He was ordained and appointed by God. He was the eternal Son of whom the Father said, "You are a priest forever" (Psalm 110:4). He made reconciliation for the people. He showed the only genuine compassion for lost mankind. The Scriptures affirm that in these qualifications as priest, Jesus our Lord became the Author, the Source, the Giver of eternal salvation.

What Jesus' manhood means to us

Let me review again what it means to us that Jesus was born into this world and lived among us. I once heard a preacher say that Jesus was man but not *a* man. I am convinced that Jesus was both man and *a* man. He had, in the most real sense, that substance and quality that is the essence of mankind. He was a man born of a woman.

Unless we understand this, I do not think we can be fully aware of what it means for Jesus to be representing us—a Man representing us at the right hand of the Majesty in the heavens. Suppose you and I were able right now to go to the presence of the Father. If we could see the Spirit, who is God, and the archangels and seraphim and strange creations out of the fire, we would see them surrounding the throne. But to our delight and amazement, we would see a Man there, human like we are—the Man Christ Jesus Himself!

Jesus, the Man who is also God, was raised as a victor from the dead and exalted to the right hand of the Father. I think it is safe to say that during this age of the work and witness of the Christian church on earth, Jesus would be the one visible Man in that heavenly company at the throne.

Of course, there are questions that students of the Bible have discussed for many years. All of us do well to confess that much about the glorious kingdom of God is yet unknown to us and cannot now be comprehended. For instance, what about the righteous dead and their place in the heaven-lies?

We might state our question like this: If the risen and glorified Jesus is ministering there, what about the great number of Christian men and women who, having died in the faith, have gone on to meet the Lord? Where are they?

First of all, and beyond any other consideration, we know that they are safely sheltered in God's heavenly realm. The apostle Paul declares that it is "better by far" for the Christian to "depart and be with Christ" (Philippians 1:23) than to continue in this world of sin and tears.

At death, only the physical body succumbs. For the believers in Christ, their undying and immortal spirits have passed into a blessed spiritual abode prepared by our God. Let us be assured that God is ever faithful in His gracious plan for His creation and for His redeemed children.

We surely know that all things are not going to continue forever as we now know them. Paul in the first century wrote advice and encouragement to the Thessalonian believers. He told them plainly that he did not want them to be unaware of the state of those believers whom he described as "asleep"—having passed into the presence of the Lord through physical death. His message was one of distinct consolation. It continues to shine as a word of hope for every believer:

We believe that Jesus died and rose again and so we believe that God will bring with Jesus those who have fallen asleep in him. According to the Lord's own word, we tell you that we

who are still alive, who are left till the coming
of the Lord, will certainly not precede those
who have fallen asleep. For the Lord himself
will come down from heaven, with a loud command, with the voice of the archangel and with
the trumpet call of God, and the dead in Christ
will rise first. After that, we who are still alive
and are left will be caught up with them in the
clouds to meet the Lord in the air. And so we
will be with the Lord forever. Therefore encour-
age each other with these words. (1 Thessalonians 4:14–18)

Plainly our Creator-God and Redeemer still has
many kingdom secrets not yet revealed to us. But
we do know that in that glad day of Christ's coming, there will be great transformations, all taking
place with split-second speed. Concerning those
great changes, Paul wrote to the Corinthian Christians:

The trumpet will sound, the dead will be raised
imperishable, and we will be changed. For the
perishable must clothe itself with the imperishable, and the mortal with immortality. (1 Corinthians 15:52–53)

Paul used the familiar analogy of plant life to describe to the Corinthians the reality of the promised
resurrection:

What you sow does not come to life unless it
dies. When you sow, you do not plant the body
that will be, but just a seed, perhaps of wheat
or of something else. But God gives it a body as
he has determined. . . .

So will it be with the resurrection of the dead. The body that is sown is perishable, it is raised imperishable; it is sown in dishonor, it is raised in glory; it is sown in weakness, it is raised in power; it is sown a natural body, it is raised a spiritual body. . . .

Just as we have borne the likeness of the earthly man, so shall we bear the likeness of the man from heaven. . . .

When the perishable has been clothed with the imperishable, and the mortal with immortality, then the saying that is written will come true: "Death has been swallowed up in victory." (1 Corinthians 15:36–38, 42–44, 49, 54)

Surely it was this same revelation by the Spirit of God that caused the writer Jude to exclaim:

To him who is able to keep you from falling and to present you before his glorious presence without fault and with great joy—to the only God our Savior be glory, majesty, power and authority, through Jesus Christ our Lord, before all ages, now and forevermore! Amen. (Jude 24–25)

We rest upon God's revelation that in the heavenly world today, Jesus in His glorified body represents us at the throne of God. Each of us who loves and serves Him has a right to the great scriptural promises. In that great climactic event of the ages, our Lord will come and we shall all be changed. He will present us before the eternal throne with exceeding joy, glorified even as He is glorified!

2

Jesus, God's Final Revelation

IT DOES NOT SPEAK too well for our Christian testimony when God tells us that He has sent His Son to be His final revelation in this world—and we act bored about it! What a gracious gesture it was on God's part. And the living God and Creator continues to speak to the men and women of a lost race:

> In the past God spoke to our forefathers through the prophets at many times and in various ways, but in these last days he has spoken to us by his Son. (Hebrews 1:1–2)

But it leaves us with some questions to answer. *Why is Christianity so boring to so many in our day? Is Jesus Christ still dead?*

"Oh, no," we are quick to reply. "He is a risen Savior." *Perhaps, then He has lost His power and His authority?*

"Of course not," we respond. "He ascended to the right hand of the Majesty on high." *Then that means He has left us to our own devices? Are we now on our own?*

"Not exactly," we answer with caution. "We really

15

have not been in very close touch with Him lately, but He is supposed to be our great High Priest at the heavenly throne."

The key to our boredom

That must be the key to our boredom with Christianity: we have not been keeping in very close touch with our Man in glory. We have been doing in our churches all those churchly things that we do. We have done them with our own understanding and in our own energy. But without a bright and conscious confirmation of God's presence, a church service can be very deadly and dull.

We go to church and we look bored—even when we are supposed to be singing God's praises. We look bored because we *are* bored. If the truth were known, we are bored with God, but we are too pious to admit it. I think God would love it if some honest soul would begin his or her prayer by admitting, "God, I am praying because I know I should, but the truth is I do not want to pray. I am bored with the whole thing!"

I doubt if the Lord would be angry at such candor. Rather, I believe He would think, "Well, there is hope for that person. That person is being truthful with Me. Most people are bored with Me and will not admit it."

Some people believe we are living in a kind of vacuum. They see this as an age in which God is not revealing Himself. They think this is an interval between the time when God spoke to mankind and the time future when He will again be a speaking God. Do you suppose they think God has become tired and is resting for a while?

No, the God who spoke in the past is speaking yet. He is speaking through the revelation of the risen and ascended Christ, the eternal Son. In all the history of God's dealings with man, there has never been an utter blackout of God's voice.

We should be thankful for this inspired letter to the Hebrews. It indicates that what God is now saying to mankind through His Son far surpasses anything in the world's great varieties of human philosophies. God's Word is not an appeal to the reasoning mind of man. It is a matter to be taken into the heart and soul.

Hebrews is a book and a message and a revelation. It stands high and lofty in its own strength because it is a fitting, forceful portrait of the eternal Son, the great High Priest of God forever and forever. I am sad because a large number of professing Christians who have tried to study the letter have finally given up. They have turned away with the very human comment, "This is too deep, too hard to understand."

We must approach the Word expectantly

I have always felt that when we read and study the Word of God we should have great expectations. We should ask the Holy Spirit to reveal the Person, the glory and the eternal ministry of our Lord Jesus Christ. Perhaps our problem is in our approach. Perhaps we have simply read our Bibles as we might read a piece of literature or a textbook.

In today's society, great numbers of people seem unable to deal with God's revelation in Christ. They run and hide, just as Adam and Eve did. Today, however, they do not hide behind trees but behind such things as philosophy and reason and even theology—believe it or not! This attitude is hard to understand.

In Jesus' death for our sins, God is offering far more than escape from a much-deserved hell. God is promising us an amazing future, an eternal future. We do not see it and understand it as we should because so much is wrong with our world. The effects of sin are all around us. The eternal purposes of God lie out yonder. I often wonder if we are making it plain enough to our generation that there will be no other revelation from God except as He speaks it through our Lord Jesus Christ.

If we have ever confessed that we need a Savior, this letter to the Hebrews should be an arresting, compelling book for us. It is a great book of redemption with an emphasis that all things in our lives must begin and end in God. As we study God's character and attributes, we will discover an important fact. Time and space, matter and motion, life and law, form and order, all purpose and all plan, all succession and all procession begin and end with God. All things move out from God and return to Him again.

I pray that God may open our eyes to see and understand that whatever does not begin in God and end in God is not worthy of any attention from man made in the image of God. We were made for God, to worship and admire and enjoy and serve Him forever.

God has always spoken to us

When the author of Hebrews wrote to declare that "in these last days" God was speaking through

His Son, he reminded us that for thousands of years God had been speaking in many ways. Actually, there had been some 4,000 years of human history during which God had been speaking to the human race. It was a race that had separated itself from God, hiding in the Garden of Eden and holding itself incognito ever since.

For most people in the first century of the Christian era, God was only a tradition. Some fondled their man-made gods. Some had ideas of worship and even built altars. Some mumbled incantations and said prayers. But they were alienated from the true God. Although they were made in the image of God, they had rejected their Creator, casting in their lot with mortality.

That situation might have continued until man or nature or both failed and were no more. But God in love and wisdom came once more. He came to speak, revealing Himself this time through His eternal Son. It is because of the coming of Jesus into the world that we now look back on the revelation in the Old Testament as fragmentary and incomplete. We could say that the Old Testament is like a house without doors and windows. Not until the carpenters cut in doors and windows can that house become a worthy, satisfying residence.

Years ago my family and I enjoyed Christian fellowship with a Jewish medical doctor who had come to personal faith in Jesus, the Savior and Messiah. He gladly discussed with me his previous participation in Sabbath services in the synagogue. Often he had been asked to read from the Old Testament Scriptures.

"I often think back on those years of reading

from the Old Testament," he told me. "I had the haunting sense that it was good and true. I knew it explained the history of my people. But I had the feeling that something was missing." Then, with a beautiful, radiant smile he added, "When I found Jesus as my personal Savior and Messiah, I found Him to be the One to whom the Old Testament was in fact pointing. I found Him to be the answer to my completion as a Jew, as a person and as a believer."

Whether Jew or Gentile, we were made originally in God's image, and the revelation of God by His Spirit is a necessity. An understanding of the Word of God must come from the same Spirit who provided its inspiration.

The purpose of Hebrews

The letter to the Hebrews was written to confirm the early Jewish Christians in their faith in Jesus, the Messiah-Savior. The writer takes a recurring theme that Jesus Christ is better because He is superior. Jesus Christ is the ultimate Word from God!

This is a reassuring, strengthening message to us in our day. Hebrews lets us know that while our Christian faith surely was foreshadowed in and grew out of Judaism, it was not and is not dependent on Judaism. The words of our Lord Jesus Christ, spoken while He was here on earth, still speak to us with spiritual authority. At one time He reminded His disciples that new wine must never be put in old, unelastic wineskins. The parable was patent: the old religious forms and traditions could never contain the new wine He was introducing.

He was saying that a fixed gulf exists between

vital Christianity and the old forms of Judaism. The Judaism of the Old Testament, with its appointed Mosaic order, had indeed mothered Christianity. But just as the child progresses to maturity and independence, so the Christian faith and the Christian evangel were independent of Judaism. Even if Judaism should cease to exist, Christianity as a revelation from God would—and does—stand firmly upon its own solid foundation. It rests upon the same living, speaking God that Judaism rested on.

It is important for us to understand that God, being one in His nature, is always able to say the same thing to everyone who hears Him. He does not have two different messages about grace or love or justice or holiness. Whether it be from the Father or the Son or the Holy Spirit, the revelation will always be the same. It points in the same direction, though using different ways and different means and different persons.

Begin in Genesis and continue through the Old and New Testaments and you will perceive the uniformity. Yet there are ever-widening elements in God's revelation to mankind. In early Genesis the Lord spoke in terms of a coming Messiah, foretelling a warfare between the serpent and the Seed of the woman. He noted the victorious Champion-Redeemer who was to come.

The Lord told Eve in very plain words of future human pain in childbearing and of woman's status in the family. He told Adam of the curse upon the ground and of inevitable death as the result of transgression. To Abel and to Cain He revealed a system of sacrifice and through it a plan of forgiveness and acceptance.

God's message to Noah was of grace and of the order of nature and government. To Abraham He gave the promise of the coming Seed, the Redeemer who would make an atonement for the race. To Moses, He gave the Law and told of the coming Prophet who was to be like Moses and yet superior to him. Those were God's spoken messages "in the past."

God's message to us

Now, what is God saying to His human creation in our day and time? In brief, He is saying, "Jesus Christ is My beloved Son. Hear Him!"

The reason many do not want to hear what God is saying through Jesus to our generation is not hard to guess. God's message in Jesus is a moral pronouncement. It brings to light such elements as faith and conscience and conduct, obedience and loyalty. Men and women reject this message for the same reason they have rejected all of the Bible. They do not wish to be under the authority of the moral Word of God.

For centuries God spoke in many ways. He inspired holy men to write portions of the message in a Book. People do not like it and try their best to avoid it because God has made it the final test of all morality, the final test of all Christian ethics.

Some are taking issue with the New Testament record. "How can you prove that Jesus actually said that?" they challenge. Perhaps they are taking issue because they have come across the unforgettable words of Jesus in John's Gospel:

As for the person who hears my words but

does not keep them, I do not judge him. For I did not come to judge the world, but to save it. There is a judge for the one who rejects me and does not accept my words; that very word which I spoke will condemn him at the last day. (John 12:47–48)

God is a living God and Jesus Christ, with all power and all authority, is at the control panel, guiding and sustaining all things in the universe. That concept is fundamental to the Christian faith. It is necessary that we really and fully comprehend that our God is indeed the Majesty in the heavens.

Hebrews reassures us

We can get this assurance from Hebrews, read in the context of the total inspired record. And as we are assured of this, we will have discovered a fundamental means of retaining our sanity in a troubled world and in a selfish society.

If we are going to keep our minds restful at all, we will actually think God into His world – not dismiss Him from His world, as many are trying to do. We will allow Him by faith to be in our beings what He actually is in His world.

The idea that God exists and that He is sovereign in the heavens is absolutely fundamental to human morality. Our view of human decency is also involved in this. Decency is that quality which is proper or becoming. Human decency depends upon an adequate and wholesome concept of God.

Those who take the position that there is no God cannot possibly hold a right and proper view of human nature. That is evident in God's revelation.

There is not a man or woman anywhere who can hold an adequate view of our human nature until he or she accepts the fact that we came from God and that we shall return to God again.

We who have admitted Jesus Christ into our lives as Savior and Lord are happy indeed that we did so. In matters of health care, we are familiar with the custom of a "second opinion." If I go to a doctor and he or she advises me to have surgery, I can leave that office and consult with another specialist about my condition. Concerning our decision to receive Jesus Christ, we surely would have been ill-advised to go out and try to get a second opinion! Jesus Christ is God's last word to us. There is no other. God has headed up all of our help and forgiveness and blessing in the person of Jesus Christ, the Son.

In our dark day, God has given us Jesus as the Light of the world. Those who refuse Him give themselves over to the outer darkness that will prevail throughout the eternal ages.

We may not like what the Great Physician tells us about ourselves and our sin. But where else can we go? Peter supplied the answer to that question. "'Lord,' he said, 'to whom shall we go? You have the words of eternal life. We believe and know that you are the Holy One of God.'"

This is the Savior whom God is offering. He is the eternal Son, equal to the Father in His Godhead, co-eternal and of one substance with the Father.

He is speaking. We should listen!

Jesus, Heir of All Things

R EBELLION AND SIN have left a monstrous blight
upon the earth that God created. But we who
have come to trust this Creator God and the written
revelation He has left for us are convinced of two
truths. One, heaven and earth are a *unity*, designed
and created by the one God. Two, this sovereign
God did not make the universe to be an everlasting
contradiction; a day of restoration lies ahead.

When we approach the letter to the Hebrews, we
discover a revealed truth within the writer's insistence that God has appointed Jesus, the eternal
Son, "through whom he made the universe," as
"heir of all things" (1:2).

With that expression, the writer is asking us to
stretch our minds and expand our understanding.
See it again: God has appointed His Son, our Lord
Jesus Christ, the One who made the worlds in
space, to be the eternal heir of "all things."

Perhaps in our day and age it does not sound
very important that Christ is the heir of all things.
That is because we may be applying our own re-
stricted meaning to the words "all things." We use
the expression to denote the circumstances of life as
they come along, easy or hard, simple or complex.
But in these opening lines of the Hebrews letter the

Holy Spirit is trying to give us a particular and significant meaning for the "all things" that are committed to Jesus Christ.

"All things" equals the universe

When the words *all things* are used in the Bible as they are found here, they are the theological equivalent of the word "universe" as used by the philosophers. Admittedly, this is not an easy concept for us to grasp. We are not used to stretching our minds! The preachers of our generation are failing us. They are not forcing us to crank up our minds and to exercise our souls in the contemplation of God's eternal themes.

Too many preachers are satisfied to dwell primarily on the escape element in Christianity. I acknowledge that the escape element is real. No one is more sure of it than I. I am going to escape a much-deserved hell because of Christ's death on the cross and His resurrection from the grave. But if we continue to emphasize that truth to the exclusion of all else, Christian believers will never fully grasp what the Scriptures are teaching us about all of the eternal purposes of God.

This same observation is true also of those who are intrigued with just the social and ethical aspects of Christianity. These may be very fulfilling and engaging, but if that is where we stop, we will never comprehend the greater promises and the loftier plans of the God who loves us and who has called us.

We must get serious

As I have said before, for a great number of unthinking people Christianity has come down to this: a nice, simple, relaxing way of having good clean fun, with the assurance that when this earthly life is over we will still go to heaven. We need to take ourselves by the scruff of the neck and vow, "I am going to think this thing through! I am going to pray through and lay hold of God's meaning for my life, for my witness and for my future!" Our Lord is trying to show us His amazing and significant plans for our eternal future.

In our relationships down here on earth, we learn of a father who has decided he will prepare an inheritance for his son. He is going to arrange for his son to come into possession of all that is in his estate: properties, bank accounts, stocks and bonds, possessions. The son will receive title to the entire estate when the inheritance becomes effective. Think of it! The son is coming into an inheritance none of which he ever owned or possessed.

But that is *not* the case with the title and possessions and authority and power of our Lord Jesus Christ. Already He is Lord. As the risen, eternal Son, He is seated in the heavenlies awaiting the day of universal consummation. In his Gospel, the apostle John has introduced us to the eternal Son, who from the beginning was the Word of God:

> In the beginning was the Word, and the Word was with God, and the Word was God. He was with God in the beginning.
> Through him all things were made; without him nothing was made that has been made. In him was life, and that life was the light of men. (John 1:1–4)

Before there was an atom or a molecule, before there was a star or a galaxy, before there was light or motion, before there was matter or mass, the eternal Son was God. He was. He existed. He would have been there even if there had not been a creation, for He was the self-existent God. Therefore, all things in all places have always belonged to Him.

God has a master plan

God is planning to do some wonderful and spectacular things with His vast creation. Paul, in his letter to the Ephesians, gave us a little glimpse into the future of the redeemed:

> He has made known to us the mystery of his will according to his good pleasure, which he purposed in Christ, to be put into effect when the times will have reached their fulfillment — to bring all things in heaven and on earth together under one head, even Christ. (Ephesians 1:9–10)

The apostle is assuring us that even as an architect-builder gathers the necessary materials needed to fashion the structure he has designed, so God will gather all things together. And how will He do that? By "bring[ing] all things in heaven and on earth together under one head, even Christ." If we will give the Scriptures attention, we will learn from them that a great future day is coming in which God will prove the essential unity of His creation. That spectacular display will be correlated and fulfilled in the person of our Lord Jesus Christ. God will make it plain that all things have derived their form from Christ; they have received their meaning by the power of His word; and they have maintained their place and order through Him.

Jesus Christ is God creating.

Jesus Christ is God redeeming.

Jesus Christ is God completing and harmonizing.

Jesus Christ is God bringing together all things after the counsel of His own will.

Not yet do we see it

After that flight of anticipation for a future still coming, I must admit that we earthbound creatures do not yet see it or sense it like that. Let me speak again of our acknowledged human shortcomings, even those that have to do with our faith. It is very hard for us to envision the risen Christ Jesus as He is now glorified at the right hand of the Majesty on high. At best "we see but a poor reflection" (1 Corinthians 13:12). At worst we are stone blind!

Not always can we see the hand of God in the things around us. We experience in this life only unfinished segments of God's great eternal plan. We do not see the hosts of heaven in the "cloud of witnesses" around us. We do not see the "spirits of righteous men made perfect" (Hebrews 12:23) or the beckoning row-on-row of principalities or the shining ranks of powers throughout the universe. In this time of our incompleteness, we do not comprehend the glory that will be ours in that future day when leaning on the arm of our heavenly Bridegroom we are led into the presence of the Father in heaven with exceeding joy.

We do our best to exercise faith. Yet we see the future consummation only dimly and imperfectly. The writer to the Hebrews has tried to help us in the proper exercise of our faith. He has done so with his amazing statement that our Lord Jesus Christ is the heir of all things in God's far-flung creation.

It is a concept having to do with everything that God has made in His vast universe. Everything has been ordered, created and laid out so that it becomes the garment of Deity or the universal living expression of Himself to the world.

When we read that God has appointed Jesus, the Son, to be the heir of all things, the reference is to the whole creation of God as it will be seen in its future, ultimate perfection. We cannot believe that God has left anything to chance in His creative scheme. That includes everything from the tiniest blade of grass on earth to the mightiest galaxy in the distant heavens above.

All things—what is included?

"Heir of all things." What does that phrase really include? It includes angels, seraphim, cherubim, ransomed men and women of all ages, matter, mind, law, spirit, value, meaning. It includes life and events on the varied levels of being. It includes all of these and more—and God's great interest embraces them all!

Are you beginning to gain a new appreciation of God's great universal purpose? I am not simply assuming the role of philosopher. The purpose of God is to *bring together*—to acquaint all rational beings with all other segments within His complex creation. I repeat that I believe in the essential unity of all God's creation. Thus, I believe a day is coming when each part of God's creation will recognize its own essential oneness with every other part. Toward that day the whole creation is moving.

When I wrote about this concept in an editorial in *Alliance Life*, a reader hastened to accuse me of being pantheistic. I am not pantheistic. And the essential unity of God's creation is not pantheism. Pantheism teaches that God is all things and that all things are God. According to pantheism, if you want to know what God is you must come to know all things. Then, if you could put all things in your arms, you would have God. Pantheism is ridiculous—claiming and teaching that all things are God.

God is imminent in His universe. That I believe. But beyond that, He is transcendent above His universe and infinitely separated from it, for He is the Creator God.

Not a new concept

These basic concepts—the mysteries of creation and God's unity forever displayed in His works—are not new. They were believed by the great Christian souls and minds of the earlier centuries. One of the notable Scottish Moravian authors was James Montgomery. Out of his writing comes this beautiful poem expressing the unity he sensed in God's creation:

> The glorious universe around,
>   The heavens with all their train,
> Sun, moon and stars are firmly bound
>   In one mysterious chain.
>
> The earth, the ocean and the sky
>   To form one world agree;

> Where all that walk or swim or fly
>   Compose one family.
>
> God in creation must display
>   His wisdom and His might;
> Where all His works with all His ways
>   Harmoniously unite.

Montgomery's use of the word *harmoniously* is impressive. It affirms that finally, when sin has been purged from God's universe, everything in creation will be consummate with everything else. There will be universal cosmic harmony.

We are only too aware that the universe as we know it is in discord. On every side sounds the raucous rattle of sin. But in that coming day sin will be purged away and all things that walk, creep, crawl, swim or fly will be found to comprise one family indeed.

And the church, too

Allow me one more point. I want to say something about the body of Christian believers and this universal unity that one day will be established in the person of Jesus Christ. If I could ask, "Do you believe in the communion of saints?" what would be your reply? Would the question make you uncomfortable?

I suspect many Protestants would chide me right here, feeling I was getting too close to doctrinal beliefs held by ecumenists or perhaps by Catholics. I am not referring to ecumenicity and dreams of organizational church union. I am gazing ahead in faith to God's great day of victory, harmony and unity, when sin is no longer present in the creation.

In that great coming day of consummation, the children of God—the believing family of God—will experience a blessed harmony and communion of the Spirit. I surely agree with the foresight of the English poet, John Brighton, who caught a glimpse of a coming day of fellowship among the people of God. He wrote:

> In one eternal bond of love,
>   One fellowship of mind,
> The saints below and saints above
>   Their bliss and glory find.

I believe that is scriptural. I do not think anyone should throw out the great doctrine of the communion of saints just because the ecumenists embrace it.

Some day we will comprehend

The unity of all things in Christ is a concept every believer should lay hold of. When we witness the future day of Christ's triumph, when He returns and we reach the consummation of all things, then we will fully comprehend the necessity for the "all things" in God's eternal plan.

Many people are having their greatest battles over their deepening sense of futility and uselessness. It is important that we grasp God's revelation that every one of us is essential to His great plan for the ages. You will seek answers in vain from fellow men and women. Seek your answers rather from God and His Word. He is sovereign; He is still running His world.

God wants us to know that He must have all the parts in order to compose His great eternal symphony. He would have us assured that each one of us is indispensable to His grand theme!

CHAPTER

4

Jesus, God's Express Image

I WISH I COULD comprehend everything that the inspired Word is trying to reveal in the statement that Jesus, the eternal Son, is the "radiance of God's glory and the exact representation of his being" (Hebrews 1:3). This much I do know and understand: *Jesus Christ is Himself God.* As a believer and a disciple, I rejoice that the risen, ascended Christ is now my High Priest and intercessor at the heavenly throne.

The writer to the Hebrews commands our attention with this descriptive, striking language:

> In these last days has spoken to us by his Son, . . . [who is] the radiance of God's glory and the exact representation of his being, sustaining all things by his powerful word. (Hebrews 1:2–3)

We trust the Scriptures because we believe they are inspired—God-breathed. Because we believe them, we believe and confess that Jesus was very God of very God.

Nothing anywhere in this vast, complex world is as beautiful and as compelling as the record of the Incarnation, the act by which God was made flesh to dwell among us in our own human history. This Jesus, the Christ of God, who made the universe

35

and who sustains all things by his powerful word, was a tiny babe among us. He was comforted to sleep when He whimpered in His mother's arms. Great, indeed, is the mystery of godliness.

Yet, in this context, some things strange and tragic have been happening in recent years within Christianity. For one, some ministers have advised their congregations not to be greatly concerned if theologians dispute the virgin birth of Jesus. The issue, they say, is not important. For another thing, some professing Christians are saying they do not want to be pinned down as to what they really believe about the uniqueness and reality of the deity of Jesus, the Christ.

We are convinced

We live in a society where we cannot always be sure that traditional definitions still hold. But I stand where I always have stood. And the genuine believer, no matter where he may be found in the world, humbly but surely is convinced about the person and position of Jesus Christ. Such a believer lives with calm and confident assurance that Jesus Christ is truly God and that He is everything the inspired writer said He is. He is "the radiance of God's glory and the exact representation of his being." This view of Christ in Hebrews harmonizes with and supports what Paul said of Jesus when he described Him as "the image of the invisible God, the firstborn over all creation" (Colossians 1:15), in whom "all the fullness of the Deity lives in bodily form" (2:9).

Bible-believing Christians stand together on this. They may have differing opinions about the mode of baptism, church polity or the return of the Lord. But they agree on the deity of the eternal Son. Jesus Christ is of one substance with the Father—begotten, not created (Nicene Creed). In our defense of this truth we must be very careful and very bold—belligerent, if need be.

The more we study the words of our Lord Jesus Christ when He lived on earth among us, the more certain we are about who He is. Some critics have protested, "Jesus did not claim to be God, you know. He only said He was the Son of Man."

It is true that Jesus used the term Son of Man frequently. If I can say it reverently, He seemed proud or at least delighted that He was a man, the Son of man. But He testified boldly, even among those who were His sworn enemies, that He was God. He said with great forcefulness that He had come from the Father in heaven and that He was equal with the Father.

We know what we believe. Let no one with soft words and charming persuasion argue us into admission that Jesus Christ is any less than very God of very God.

God became flesh in Jesus Christ

The writer of Hebrews was informing the persecuted, discouraged Jewish Christians concerning God's final and complete revelation in Jesus Christ. He spoke of the God of Abraham, Isaac and Jacob. Then he declared that Another had come. Although made flesh, He was none other than this same God. Not the Father, for God the Father was never incarnated and never will be. Rather, He is

God the eternal Son, the radiance of the Father's glory and the exact representation of His being.

Something has happened to the word *glory*, especially as it relates to the description of deity. Glory is one of those beautiful, awesome words that have been dragged down until they have lost much of their meaning. The old artists may have had something to do with it, depicting the glory of Jesus Christ as a luminous halo—a shining neon hoop around His head. But the glory of Jesus Christ was never a luminous ring around the head. It was never a misty yellow light.

We are inclined to irreverence

I have a difficult time excusing our careless and irreverent attitudes concerning our Lord and Savior. I feel strongly that worshiping Christians should never be guilty of using a theological word or expression in a popular or careless sense unless we explain what we are doing. It is only proper when we speak of the glory of God the Son to actually refer to that uniqueness of His person and character that excites our admiration and wonder.

To those who love this One and serve Him, His glory does not mean yellow light or neon hoops. His true glory is that which causes the heavenly beings to cover their faces in His presence. It brings forth their worshipful praise: "Holy, holy, holy is the Lord God of hosts!" The glory of the Lord is that forth-shining that gives Him universal praise. It demands love and worship from His created beings. It makes Him known throughout His creation.

It is the character of God that is the glory of God.

God is not glorified until men and women think gloriously of Him. Yet it is not what people think of God that matters. God once dwelt in light which no one could approach. But He desired to speak, to express Himself. So He created the heavens and the earth, filling earth with His creatures, including mankind. He expected man to respond to that in Him which is glorious, admirable and excellent.

That response from His creation in love and worship is His glory. When we say that Christ is the radiance of God's glory, we are saying that Christ is the shining forth of all that God is. Yes, He is the shining forth, the effulgence. When God expressed Himself, it was in Christ Jesus. Christ was all and in all. He is the exact representation of God's person.

"Exact representation," "person"

The word *person* in this context is difficult of comprehension. Church history testifies to the difficulties theologians have had with it. Sometimes the *person* of God has been called substance. Sometimes it has been called essence. The Godhead cannot be comprehended by the human mind. But the eternal God sustains, upholds, stands beneath all that composes the vast created universe. And Jesus Christ has been presented to us as the exact representation of God's *person*—all that God is.

The words *exact representation*, of course, have their origin in the pressed-upon-wax seal that authenticated a dignitary's document or letter. The incarnate Jesus Christ gives visible shape and authenticity to deity. When the invisible God became visible, He was Jesus Christ. When the God who could not be seen or touched came to dwell among us, He was Jesus Christ.

I have not suggested this picture of our Lord Jesus Christ as a kind of theological argument. I am simply trying to state, in the best way I can, what the Holy Spirit has spoken through the consecrated writer of the letter to the Hebrews.

What is God like?

What is God like? Throughout the ages, that question has been asked by more people than any other. Our little children are only a few years old when they come in their innocent simplicity and inquire of us, "What is God like?" Philip the apostle asked it for himself and for all mankind: "'Show us the Father and that will be enough for us'" (John 14:8). Philosophers repeatedly have asked the question. Religionists and thinkers have wrestled with it for milleniums.

Paul preached at Athens and spoke of mankind's quest for the "Unknown God." He declared God's intention that mankind "'would seek him and perhaps reach out for him and find him, though he is not far from each one of us. "For in him we live and move and have our being"'" (Acts 17:27–28). Paul was speaking about the presence of God in the universe—a Presence that becomes the living, vibrant voice of God causing the human heart to reach out after Him. Alas! Man has not known where to reach because of sin. Sin has blinded his eyes, dulled his hearing and made his heart unresponsive.

Sin has made man like a bird without a tongue. It has within itself the instinct and the desire to sing, but not the ability. The poet Keats expressed beautifully, even brilliantly, the fantasy of the nightingale that had lost its tongue. Not being able to express the deep instinct to sing, the bird died of an overpowering suffocation within.

Eternity in our hearts

God made mankind in His own image. He "set eternity in the hearts of men" (Ecclesiastes 3:11). What a graphic picture! How much it explains ourselves to us! We are creatures of time—time in our hands, our feet, our bodies—that causes us to grow old and to die. Yet all the while we have eternity in our hearts!

One of our great woes as fallen people living in a fallen world is the constant warfare between the eternity in our hearts and the time in our bodies. This is why we can never be satisfied without God. This is why the question "What is God like?" continues to spring from every one of us. God has set the values of eternity in the hearts of every person made in His image.

As human beings, we have ever tried to satisfy ourselves by maintaining a quest, a search. We have not forgotten that God *was*. We have only forgotten what God is like.

Philosophy has tried to give us answers. But the philosophical concepts concerning God have always been contradictory. The philosopher is like a blind person trying to paint someone's portrait. The blind person can feel the face of his subject and try to put some brush strokes on canvas. But the project is doomed before it is begun. The best that philosophy can do is to feel the face of the universe in some ways, then try to paint God as philosophy sees Him.

Most philosophers confess belief in a "presence" somewhere in the universe. Some call it a "law" — or "energy" or "mind" or "essential virtue." Thomas Edison said if he lived long enough, he thought he could invent an instrument so sensitive that it could find God. Edison was an acknowledged inventor. He had a great mind and he may have been a philosopher. But Edison knew no more about God or what God is like than the boy or girl who delivers the morning newspaper.

Religions have no answers

The religions of the world have always endeavored to give answers concerning God. The Parsees, for example, declare that God is light. So they worship the sun and fire and forms of light. Other religions have suggested that God is conscience, or that He may be found in virtue. For some religions, there is solace in the belief that God is a principle upholding the universe.

There are religions that teach that God is all justice. They live in terror. Others say that God is all love. They become arrogant. Like the philosophers, religionists have concepts and views, ideas and theories. In none of them has mankind found satisfaction.

Greek paganism had a pantheon of gods. They saw the sun rising in the east and moving westward in a blaze of fire and called it Apollo. They heard the wind roaring along the sea coast and named her Eos, mother of the winds and the stars. They saw the waters of the ocean churning themselves into foam and named him Neptune. They imagined a goddess hovering over the fruitful fields of grain each year and gave her the name Ceres.

Given such a pagan outlook, there is no end to the fantasies of gods and goddesses. In Romans 1 God has described the human condition that incubates such aberrations. Men and women, intrigued by their sin, did not want the revelation of a living, speaking God. They deliberately ignored the only true God, crowded Him out of their lives. In His place they invented gods of their own: birds and animals and reptiles.

Often enough we have been warned that the morality of any nation or civilization will follow its concepts of God. A parallel truth is less often heard: When a church begins to think impurely and inadequately about God, decline sets in.

We must think nobly and speak worthily of God. Our God is sovereign. We would do well to follow our old-fashioned forebears who knew what it was to kneel in breathless, wondering adoration in the presence of the God who is willing to claim us as His own through grace.

Jesus is what God is like

Some are still asking, "What is God like?" God Himself has given us a final, complete answer. Jesus said, "'Anyone who has seen me has seen the Father,'" (John 14:9).

For those of us who have put our faith in Jesus Christ, the quest of the ages is over. Jesus Christ, the eternal Son, came to dwell among us, being "the radiance of God's glory and the exact representation of his being." For us, I say, the quest is over because God has now revealed Himself to us. What Jesus is, the Father is. Whoever looks on the Lord Jesus Christ looks upon all of God. Jesus is God thinking God's thoughts. Jesus is God feeling the way God feels. Jesus is God now doing what God does.

In John's Gospel, we have the record of Jesus telling the people of His day that He could do nothing of Himself. He said, "'The Son can do nothing by himself; he can do only what he sees his Father doing, because whatever the Father does the Son also does'" (John 5:19). It was on the strength of such testimony that the Jewish leaders wanted to stone Him for blasphemy.

How strange it is that some of the modern cults try to tell us that Jesus Christ never claimed to be God. Yet those who heard Him 2,000 years ago wanted to kill Him on the spot because He claimed to be one with the Father.

In Jesus the revelation is complete

God's revelation of Himself is complete in Jesus Christ, the Son. No longer need we ask, "What is God like?" Jesus is God. He has translated God into terms we can understand.

We know how He feels toward a fallen woman: "'Neither do I condemn you,' Jesus declared. 'Go now and leave your life of sin'" (John 8:11).

We know how He feels toward fishermen and workmen and common people: "'Come, follow me,' Jesus said, 'and I will make you fishers of men'" (Mark 1:17).

We know what God thinks of babies and little

children: "Jesus said, 'Let the little children come to me, and do not hinder them, for the kingdom of heaven belongs to such as these'" (Matthew 19:14).

Jesus has been in our world. He spoke and taught about all these things and about everything that concerns us. The record shows that His listeners were amazed and astonished, almost to the point of being frightened. "The crowds were amazed at his teaching, because he taught as one who had authority" (Matthew 7:28–29). "'No one ever spoke the way this man does'" (John 7:46).

When you read your New Testament and realize afresh the attitudes and the utterances of our Lord Jesus Christ, you will know exactly how God feels. Where can we look in all the vast creation around us to find anything as beautiful—as utterly, awesomely, deeply beautiful—as the Incarnation? God became flesh to dwell among us, to redeem us, to restore us, to save us completely. Young or old or in between, we join in Lowell Mason's hymn of praise:

> O could I speak the matchless worth,
> O could I sound the glories forth
>   Which in my Savior shine,
> I'd soar and touch the heavenly strings,
> And vie with Gabriel while he sings
>   In notes almost divine.
>
> I'd sing the characters He bears,
> And all the forms of love He wears,
>   Exalted on His throne:
> In loftiest songs of sweetest praise,
> I would to everlasting days
>   Make all His glories known.

There is a closing stanza which anticipates the welcome we shall receive in heaven and the everlasting career awaiting us there:

Soon the delightful day will come
When my dear Lord will bring me home,
    And I shall see His face:
Then with my Savior, Brother, Friend,
A blest eternity I'll spend,
    Triumphant in His grace.

The convinced man who breathed those words was saying that Jesus is God! And the world above and the poorer world beneath join in response: "Amen, amen! Jesus is God!"

Jesus, Lord of the Angels

OUR PROTESTANT CHURCHES have never been very enthusiastic about the Bible references to the many kinds of angels and angelic beings which make up the Lord's heavenly host. Because we do not see them, we generally do not discuss them. There seem to be many Christians who are not sure what they should believe about God's heavenly messengers.

In short, where the matter of Bible teaching about angels is concerned, we have come into a sad state of neglect and ignorance.

Personally, I despise the cynical references to angels and the comic jokes about them. The preacher who reported his guardian angel had had a hard time keeping up with him as he sped over the highway spoke in bad taste and probably in ignorance. If that is the best a preacher can say about the guardian angels or God's angelic host, he needs to go back to his Bible.

The writer of the letter to the Hebrews gives his readers a vivid, vital portrait of Jesus, the eternal Son. He knows their familiarity, through the Old Testament, with the concept and ministry of angels. He trades on that knowledge to point out the

overwhelming superiority of the victorious Jesus as
He ministers in the heavenly world above:

> Again, when God brings his first-born into the
> world, he says,
>   "Let all God's angels worship him."
> In speaking of the angels he says,
>   "He makes his angels winds,
>   his servants flames of fire."
> But about the Son he says,
>   "Your throne, O God, will last for ever and
> ever,
>   and righteousness will be the scepter of
> your kingdom." (Hebrews 1:6–8)

In this revealing comparison between angels and
the Messiah-Savior, Jesus Christ, we need to bear
in mind that the ministries of angels were very well
known and highly respected among the Jews. It
should be of great significance to us, then, that the
writer would assure them that Jesus our Lord is
infinitely above and superior to the brightest angels
who inhabit the kingdom of God. Never has there
been a created angelic being of whom it could be
said, as it was said of Christ, He is "the radiance of
God's glory and the exact representation of his
being" (1:3).

The readers needed encouragement

This full-orbed vision of the glories and creden-
tials of Jesus Christ was needed just then by the
persecuted Hebrew Christians. And to us in this
20th century of the Christian church, the same revelation comes with God's authority and meaning.
The word that assured the Hebrews reveals to us

that the eternal Son was preeminent above Abraham, above Moses, above Aaron and the priests of the Old Testament era.

Much of our Bible study tends to be one-sided. We choose to read what we like. We neglect those portions that seem to have less interest for us. Do you agree?

Among Protestant Christians for several years there has been a rather mystifying psychology. Our Roman Catholic neighbors in their hymnody and teaching have given considerable recognition to the holy angels. Protestants seem to have reacted in a reverse way. It is as though we have decided to say nothing at all about the angels.

In Old Testament times and in the early Christian church, there were churchmen and scholars who gave much attention to matters relating to angelic hosts and their appearance. When Paul spoke of the creation to the Colossians, he mentioned both the visible and the invisible world, naming thrones, powers, rulers, authorities (Colossians 1:16). Often these have been perceived of as ranks or degrees of angelic beings and their authority and power.

Paul mentioned the existence of archangels in the heavens when he wrote to the Thessalonians. "The Lord himself will come down from heaven, with a loud command, with the voice of the archangel" (1 Thessalonians 4:16). No, we are not prepared to argue against the reality of either the visible or the invisible world. Because the religion of the Hebrews was divinely given, it reflected the two worlds accurately.

Science demands measurable evidence

Consider why we think like we do in today's society. We are participants in a new age—a scientific age, an atomic age, a space age. We have been conditioned by our sciences. No longer have we any great sense of wonder or appreciation for what God continues to do in His creation. Amid our complex engineering and technological accomplishments, it is difficiult for us to look out on God's world as we should.

As believers in God and in His plan for mankind, we must not yield to the philosophies that surround us. We have a God-given message to proclaim to our generation: *The world was made by Almighty God.* It bears the stamp of deity upon it and within it.

An architect leaves his stamp upon the great buildings he has designed. A notable artist leaves his mark and personality on his paintings. The same principle applies to the visible and invisible worlds. We call them two worlds, although probably they are but one. God's stamp as designer and creator is there, just as His own mark and personality can be found throughout the sacred Scriptures.

God has told us much about His invisible world and kingdom. In that telling He has revealed many things about the heavenly beings that do His will.

Angels are an order of transcendent beings. They are shown to be holy and they are shown to be sexless. Jesus in His earthly ministry, speaking of the resurrection and the coming kingdom, said that we will be without sexual identification in that heavenly abode—"'like the angels'" (Mark 12:25).

But we will not become angels in the life to come, contrary to what some have believed since childhood. God makes it clear that we do not change from one species to another. We are redeemed human beings, and we look forward in faith to the day of our resurrection and glorification as redeemed human beings. Angels are one order of created being; humans are another (Hebrews 2:16).

Angels and Christmas

We are probably most familiar with angels as a result of the Christmas story. They heralded Jesus' birth. "Suddenly a great company of the heavenly host appeared with the angel, praising God . . ." (Luke 2:13). Jesus Himself spoke of "legions" of angels. "'Do you think I cannot call on my Father, and he will at once put at my disposal more than twelve legions of angels?'" (Matthew 26:53). The writer to the Hebrews refers to their number as "thousands upon thousands" (Hebrews 12:22). And David the psalmist refers to "the chariots of God" as numbering "tens of thousands / and thousands of thousands" (Psalm 68:17). No one is able to answer conclusively why God made the heavenly host so numerous.

Going back into the Old Testament, we note that angels apparently had some function at the creation. In His conversation with Job, God spoke of laying earth's "cornerstone" and remarked that "all the angels shouted for joy" (Job 38:7). Angels figured in the giving of the Law at Sinai. "The law," wrote the apostle Paul, "was put into effect through angels by a mediator" (Galatians 3:19).

An angel—Gabriel by name—appeared to the virgin Mary with the announcement that she would give birth to a Son whom she was to name Jesus (Luke 1:26–31). In telling the story of Lazarus, the destitute beggar, Jesus declared that "angels carried him to Abraham's side" (Luke 16:22). It is a picture almost reminiscent of the "ticker tape" parades welcoming our nation's heroes. That righteous beggar was escorted into the precincts of heaven with the angels leading the procession. I am convinced that the angels of God have a large role in preserving the righteous.

Although most of us do not talk about it, Jesus said of the children, "Their angels in heaven always see the face of my Father in heaven" (Matthew 18:10).

In all that Jesus said about angels, no words are more significant for us members of a fallen race than His statement that "there is rejoicing in the presence of the angels of God over one sinner who repents" (Luke 15:10).

We read with tender feeling of Jesus' agony and stress as He prayed in the Garden of Gethsemane. When He had prayed to the point of exhaustion as He faced betrayal and the coming crucifixion, "an angel from heaven appeared to him and strengthened him" (Luke 22:43).

At Jesus' resurrection, angels were much in evidence. An angel rolled the stone from the tomb's entrance. Angels announced to Jesus' distraught followers the joyful tidings of His resurrection.

Anyone who wants to can put a film of unbelief over his or her eyes and thus deny the existence and activity of angels. But in doing so, he or she is denying clear biblical teaching.

Some protest the discussion of angels, saying, "Let's be practical!" By which they mean, "Let's limit our considerations to three-dimensional, sense-perceived objects." There is a day coming when the answers to our questions will be plain. On that day we will discover that the ministries of the angelic beings are indeed practical and very real.

I have never seen an angel

Now, you probably are wondering how much personal experience I have had with angelic beings. "Have I ever seen an angel?"

I have never seen an angel. Nor have I ever claimed to be a visionary person. My calling has been to pray and study and to try to find from the Scriptures what God is doing and what He has promised to do. I proclaim the teaching of the Scriptures that the angels of God are busy in their special ministries. I base that observation on the Word of God, not upon any facet of my own human experience.

The Bible does not tell any of us to spend our time trying to get in touch with angels. It does tell us that angels exist and that they are busy. Their activity is frequently mentioned in the Scriptures. I am not going to skip over those references, ignoring them, as some do.

At times we talk about the providential care of God without really knowing what we say and what we mean. Some Christians testify to "coincidences" in their lives—perhaps two very important things occurring at just the right time and place. Hundreds of years ago Thomas Aquinas wrote to the Christian church, saying, "The function of God's angels is to execute the plan of divine providence, even in earthly things." Then John Calvin followed with his teaching that "angels are the dispensers and administrators of the divine beneficence toward us."

God has His own ways and means of working out His plans on behalf of His believing children. We ought not to ask the Lord for a printed list of rules about His providences and guidance. As we trust in the Spirit, live in the Spirit and walk in the Spirit, we will realize that God is always on our side.

Angels in disguise

This was true in my own experience. After I had found the Lord as a youth, I was attending a church that seemed to be of very little spiritual help to me. Actually, it was the kind of church in which it would be easy to backslide. One Sunday morning I awoke in a bad mood. "I am not going to church today!" I decided. So I went for a walk in the country. I did not have any golf clubs to use as an excuse. Neither did I tell the Lord I was going to worship amid the beauties of nature. I knew within myself that I really was backsliding—going in the wrong direction that Sunday morning.

I turned aside to walk through a grassy field. In the middle of the field my foot suddenly kicked something hidden in the grass—something red. I stooped and picked up an old red-bound book. It looked as if it had been in the rain, had dried out, had been rained on again and dried out again. The book was not some old literary classic. It was not a discarded book of cheap fiction. It was a Christian handbook: a thousand questions and answers for anyone interested in Bible study.

I opened it. And after I had scanned a few pages of biblical teaching, I became impressed by the fact that I should have been in church with other believers that morning. I threw the book back on the ground and started for home, wondering who had put such a message directly in the way of a discouraged Christian boy who was too gloomy to go to church.

I am not saying that the book was placed there by an angel or some other heavenly visitor in just the right spot. In all likelihood it was dropped in that place by someone who had chanced to pass through the field. But in the providence of God it was that day the reminder I needed of the goodness and faithfulness of God in my life.

I recall still another personal experience during my early Christian life as an unsettled young man. Actually, I was doing some "bumming around," as we used to say. I was away from home, away from the church and away from everything that was right. I would spend weekends "riding the rods." I had little money, and I would hitch free rides on the freight trains, riding the rods under the boxcars.

The Lord chose a particular Sunday to teach me the lesson I had to learn. I do not remember now which town was involved, but *I* was involved and so was the Lord. The freight train slowed down, then braked to a stop. The car that I was riding halted directly alongside a church yard. The train had hardly stopped when the church bells began to ring. They rang more loudly and more insistently than any bells I have heard before or since!

I have sat under strong preaching, but never has a preacher laid conviction on my soul like those church bells did that Sunday morning. I do not know if they were Methodist or Presbyterian or Anglican church bells. But they reminded me that I should not be riding freight trains. Rather, I should be back where I belonged. And, believe me, very soon I was back where I belonged—and straightened out spiritually, too!

How was all of that arranged? The right day, the right hour, the right place. If I had walked up to the engineer to inquire if he was an angel, he probably would have smiled, spit some tobacco juice over the cab window sill and replied, "Not that I know of!" But this I am sure of: when that engineer put on those brakes, it was by the providence of God that I would be halted practically in a church yard, with the bells pleading, "Go back, young man! Go back, young man."

God knows us well

My point is that God knows us so well that He does a number of little providential things at the very moment of our need. We think we have planned and executed everything all by ourselves. We are not aware that it has been God's plan and that He has been out there ahead of us the whole time.

It was some years later, as I read Psalm 71 in the familiar King James Version, that I noticed for the first time the words, "Thou hast given commandment to save me" (71:2). My heart has been warm ever since with that thought. God has sent His Word throughout all of the earth to save me. You may be critical if you wish. Do with that text as you will. You may even have some theological problem with it. But God has "given commandment," and these words are for me!

God saw me, a lonely, lost boy in rural western Pennsylvania, and His commandment went throughout His creation. I am convinced every angel in heaven heard it. And I believed on the Son of God and turned myself over to Him for salvation!

Nothing can compare with this knowledge. God and His Word are on my side. The living Word of God has charged Himself with the responsibility to forgive me, to cleanse me, to perfect that which concerns me and to keep me in the way everlasting.

We are living in a world full of God's created beings—many of them not seen by us or those around us. We ought to thank God for the angels and for God's providential circumstances every day. As one of the old saints long ago remarked, "If you will thank God for your providences, you will never lack a providence to thank God for!"

CHAPTER

6

Jesus, Standard of Righteousness

THE MESSAGE TO FIRST CENTURY Hebrew Christians was precise and direct: Let Jesus Christ be your motivation to love righteousness and to hate iniquity. In our present century our spiritual obligations and responsibilities are no different. The character and attributes of Jesus, the eternal Son, have not changed and will not change.

> But about the Son he says,
> "Your throne, O God, will last for ever and ever,
> and righteousness will be the scepter of your kingdom.
> You have loved righteousness and hated wickedness;
> therefore God, your God, has set you above your companions
> by anointing you with the oil of joy." (Hebrews 1:8–9)

Without excuse

There is a tendency for people to relegate everything in the realm of righteousness or iniquity to deity, whatever their concept of deity may be. For

59

the true Christian, however, our risen Lord made a promise to us before His death and resurrection. That promise effectively removes our excuses and makes us responsible:

> When he, the Spirit of truth, comes, he will guide you into all truth. He will not speak on his own; he will speak only what he hears, and he will tell you what is yet to come. He will bring glory to me by taking from what is mine and making it known to you. All that belongs to the Father is mine. That is why I said the Spirit will take from what is mine and make it known to you. (John 16:13–15)

I will readily admit that we are not God. We cannot do in ourselves what God can do. But God created us as human beings, and if we have the anointing of the Holy Spirit and His presence in our lives, we should be able to do what Jesus, the Son of Man, was able to do in His earthly ministry.

Please do not close this book and turn away when I tell you of my persuasion. I am persuaded that our Lord Jesus, while He was on earth, did not accomplish His powerful deeds in the strength of His deity. I believe He did them in the strength and authority of His Spirit-anointed humanity.

My reasoning is this: If Jesus had come to earth and performed His ministry in the power of His deity, what He did would have been accepted as a matter of course. Cannot God do anything He wants to do? No one would have questioned His works as the works of deity. But Jesus veiled His deity and ministered as a man. It is noteworthy, however, that He did not begin His ministry—His deeds of authority and power—until He had been anointed with the Holy Spirit.

I know there are erudite scholars and theological experts who will dispute my conclusion. Nevertheless, I hold it true. Jesus Christ, in the power and authority of His Spirit-anointed humanity, stilled the waves, quieted the winds, healed the sick, gave sight to the blind, exercised complete authority over demons and raised the dead. He did all the miraculous things He was moved to do among men not as God, which would not have been miraculous at all, but as a Spirit-anointed man. Remarkable!

This is why I say that Jesus Christ has taken away our human excuses forever. He limited Himself to the same power available to any one of us, the power of the Holy Spirit. Review with me the message of the apostle Peter to Cornelius and his Gentile household:

> God anointed Jesus of Nazareth with the Holy Spirit and power, . . . he went around doing good and healing all who were under the power of the devil, because God was with him. (Acts 10:38)

The letter to the Hebrews says the anointing God placed upon Jesus was an anointing above His fellows. It is my feeling that the "anointing above His fellows" was not given because God chose to so anoint Him, but because He was willing. He could be anointed to that extent!

What did the anointing signify?

Going back into the Levitical priesthood, we discover a ritual of an anointing with a specially prepared holy oil. Certain pungent herbs were beaten into the oil, making it fragrant and aromatic. It was unique; Israel might not use that formula for any other oil. When a priest was set apart and anointed, the oil was a vivid type of the New Testament anointing of the Holy Spirit. The holy anointing oil could only be used for the anointing of men with special ministries—priests, as I have indicated, and kings and prophets. It was not intended for the carnal, sinful person.

In Leviticus we read of the consecration of Aaron as the first high priest. The anointing oil and the blood from the altar are mentioned together: "Moses took some of the anointing oil and some of the blood from the altar and sprinkled them on Aaron and his garments. . . . So he consecrated Aaron and his garments" (8:30).

The fragrance of the anointing oil was unique. If someone went near an Old Testament priest, he could say immediately, "I smell an anointed man. I smell the holy oil!" The aroma, the pungency, the fragrance were there. Such an anointing could not be kept a secret.

In the New Testament, when the Holy Spirit came, His presence fulfilled that whole list of fragrances found in the holy anointing oil. When New Testament believers were anointed, that anointing was evident. Read it in the book of Acts. "All of them were filled with the Holy Spirit" (Acts 2:4). "And they were all filled with the Holy Spirit and spoke the word of God boldly" (4:31). "Stephen, full of the Holy Spirit, looked up to heaven" (7:55). "While Peter was still speaking these words, the

Holy Spirit came on all who heard the message"
(10:44). The list goes on.

The Holy Spirit has not changed. His power and
authority have not changed. He is still the third
Person of the eternal Godhead. He is among us to
teach us all we need to know about Jesus Christ,
the eternal Son of God.

I am suggesting—indeed, I am stating—that no
one among us, man or woman, can be genuinely
anointed with the Holy Spirit and hope to keep it a
secret. His or her anointing will be evident.

The anointing is no secret

A Christian brother once confided in me how he
had tried to keep the fullness of the Spirit a secret
within his own life. He had made a commitment of
his life to God in faith. In answer to prayer, God
had filled him with the Spirit. Within himself he
said, "I cannot tell anyone about this!"

Three days passed. On the third day his wife
touched him on the arm and asked, "Everett, what
has happened to you? Something has happened to
you!" And like a pent-up stream his testimony
flowed out. He had received an anointing of the
Holy Spirit. The fragrance could not be hidden. His
wife knew it in the home. His life was changed.
The spiritual graces and fruits of the consecrated
life cannot be hidden. It is an anointing with the oil
of gladness and joy.

I am happy to tell everyone that the power of the
Spirit is glad power! Our Savior, Jesus Christ, lived
His beautiful, holy life on earth and did His heal-
ing, saving deeds of power in the strength of this
oil of gladness.

We must admit that there was more of the holy oil of God on the head of Jesus than on your head or mine—or on the head of anyone else who has ever lived. That is not to say that God will withhold His best from anyone. But the Spirit of God can only anoint in proportion to the willingness He finds in our lives. In the case of Jesus, we are told that He had a special anointing because He loved righteousness and hated iniquity. That surely gives us the clue we need concerning the kind of persons we must be in order to receive the full anointing and blessing from Almighty God.

When Jesus was on earth, He was not the passive, colorless, spineless person He is sometimes made out to be in paintings and literature. He was a strong man, a man of iron will. He was able to love with an intensity of love that burned Him up. He was able to hate with the strongest degree of hatred against everything that was wrong and evil and selfish and sinful.

Invariably someone will object when I make a statement like that. "I cannot believe such things about Jesus. I always thought it was a sin to hate!"

Study long and well the record and the teachings of Jesus while He was on earth. In them lies the answer. It is a sin for the children of God *not* to hate what ought to be hated. Our Lord Jesus loved righteousness, but He hated iniquity. I think we can say He hated sin and wrong and evil perfectly!

We must hate some things

If we are committed, consecrated Christians, truly disciples of the crucified and risen Christ, there are some things we must face.

We cannot love honesty without hating dishonesty.

We cannot love purity without hating impurity.

We cannot love truth without hating lying and deceitfulness.

If we belong to Jesus Christ, we must hate evil even as He hated evil in every form. The ability of Jesus Christ to hate that which was against God and to love that which was full of God was the force that made Him able to receive the anointing – the oil of gladness – in complete measure. On our human side, it is our imperfection in loving the good and hating the evil that prevents us from receiving the Holy Spirit in complete measure. God withholds from us because we are unwilling to follow Jesus in His great poured-out love for what is right and His pure and holy hatred of what is evil.

Hate sin but love the sinner

This question always arises: "Did our Lord Jesus Christ hate sinners?" We already know the answer. He loved the world. We know better than to think that Jesus hated any sinner.

Jesus never hated a sinner, but He hated the evil and depravity that controlled the sinner. He did not hate the proud Pharisee, but He detested the pride and self-righteousness of the Pharisee. He did not hate the woman taken in adultery. But he acted against the harlotry that made her what she was.

Jesus hated the devil and He hated those evil spirits that He challenged and drove out. We present-day Christians have been misled and brainwashed, at least in a general way, by a generation of soft, pussycat preachers. They would have us believe that to be good Christians we must be able to purr softly and accept everything that comes along with Christian tolerance and understanding. Such ministers never mention words like *zeal* and *conviction* and *commitment*. They avoid phrases like "standing for the truth."

I am convinced that a committed Christian will show a zealous concern for the cause of Christ. He or she will live daily with a set of spiritual convictions taken from the Bible. He or she will be one of the toughest to move—along with a God-given humility—in his or her stand for Christ. Why, then, have Christian ministers so largely departed from exhortations to love righteousness with a great, overwhelming love, and to hate iniquity with a deep, compelling revulsion?

Why no persecution?

People remark how favored the church is in this country. It does not have to face persecution and rejection. If the truth were known, our freedom from persecution is because we have taken the easy, the popular way. If we would love righteousness until it became an overpowering passion, if we would renounce everything that is evil, our day of popularity and pleasantness would quickly end. The world would soon turn on us.

We are too nice! We are too tolerant! We are too anxious to be popular! We are too quick to make excuses for sin in its many forms! If I could stir Christians around me to love God and hate sin, even to the point of being a bit of a nuisance, I would rejoice. If some Christian were to call me for counsel saying he or she is being persecuted for

Jesus' sake, I would say with feeling, "Thank God!"

Vance Havner used to remark that too many are running for something when they ought to be standing for something. God's people should be willing to stand! We have become so brainwashed in so many ways that Christians are afraid to speak out against uncleanness in any form. The enemy of our souls has persuaded us that Christianity should be a rather casual thing—certainly not something to get excited about.

Fellow Christian, we only have a little time. We are not going to be here very long. Our triune God demands that we engage in those things that will remain when the world is on fire, for fire determines the value and quality of every person's work.

I have shared these things with you because I am of the opinion that the glad oil, the blessed anointing of the Holy Spirit, is not having opportunity to flow freely among church members of our day. We can hardly expect any such spiritual movement among those who proudly class themselves as liberals. They reject the deity of Christ, the inspiration of the Bible and the divine ministries of the Holy Spirit. How can the oil of God flow among and bless those who do not believe in such an oil of gladness?

But what about us of the evangelical persuasion with our biblical approach to fundamental New Testament truth and teaching? We must ask ourselves why the oil of God is not flowing very noticeably around us. We have the truth. We believe in the anointing and the unction. Why is the oil not flowing?

We are tolerant of evil

I think the reason is that we are tolerant of evil. We allow what God hates because we want to be known to the world as good-natured, agreeable Christians. Our stance indicates that the last thing we would want anyone to say about us is that we are narrow-minded.

The way to spiritual power and favor with God is to be willing to put away the weak compromises and the tempting evils to which we are prone to cling. There is no Christian victory or blessing if we refuse to turn away from the things that God hates.

Even if your wife loves it, turn away from it.

Even if your husband loves it, turn away from it.

Even if it is accepted in the whole social class and system of which you are a part, turn away from it.

Even if it is something that has come to be accepted by our whole generation, turn away from it if it is evil and wrong and an offense to our holy and righteous Savior.

I am being as frank and as searching as I can possibly be. I know that we lack the courage and the gladness that should mark the committed people of God. And that concerns me. Deep within the human will with which God has endowed us, every Christian holds the key to his or her own spiritual attainment. If he or she will not pay the price of being joyfully led by the Holy Spirit of God, if he or she refuses to hate sin and evil and wrong, our churches might as well be turned into lodges or clubs.

O brother, sister! God has not given up loving us. The Holy Spirit still is God's faithful Spirit. Our

Lord Jesus Christ is at the right hand of the Majesty in heaven, representing us there, interceding for us. God is asking us to stand in love and devotion to Him. The day is coming when judgment fire tries every person's work. The hay, wood and stubble of worldly achievement will be consumed. God wants us to know the reward of gold and silver and precious stones.

Following Jesus Christ is serious business. Let us quit being casual about heaven and hell and the judgment to come!

Jesus, the Eternal Word

T HE INSPIRED MESSAGE nearly 2,000 years ago to the hard-pressed Hebrew Christians was a moving appeal to place their full confidence in the power of the Word of God. When God speaks, the writer said in effect, all must obey. The writer declared:

> The word of God is living and active. Sharper than any double-edged sword, it penetrates even to dividing soul and spirit, joints and marrow; it judges the thoughts and attitudes of the heart. (Hebrews 4:12)

That same message continues throughout the letter with reminders of the relationship of God's Word to the universe of which we are a part. We are told of God's Word sounding throughout all of God's creation, keeping, sustaining, transforming.

The Word of God is more than just the Bible

Christian believers make a great mistake when they refer only to the Bible as the Word of God. True, the inspired Bible is the Word of God speaking to our hearts and to our souls. But in referring to the Word of God, we do not mean just the book—printed pages sewed together with nylon thread. Rather, we mean the eternal expression of the mind of God. We mean the world-filling breath of God!

God's Word and God's revelation are much more than just the Old and New Testament books. Nevertheless I invariably rejoice as I discover deep in the urgent appeal of one of the Old Testament prophets a sudden recognition of God's speaking Word. For example, notice this message from the prophet Jermiah: "O land, land, land, / hear the word of the Lord!" (Jeremiah 22:29).

Think what a change it would make in the world if men and women suddenly paused to hear the Word of the Lord! The Word of God being what it is, and God being who He is, and we humans being who we are, I am sure that the most rewarding thing we could do would be to stop and listen to the Word of God. Whether a man or a woman believes it or not, the Word of God is one of the greatest of the realities he or she will face in a lifetime. He or she may deny the Word and the presence of God, dismissing them both as unreal. But the living, speaking Word of God cannot be escaped. Neither is it negotiable.

The true Christian church has always held that position. There is not a man or woman on the face of the earth but will have to reckon with the authority of the Word of God, either now or later. How surprised some of them will be on that coming day of judgment when God's eternal Word must be answered to!

God's Word is the revelation of divine truth that God Himself has given to us. It has come in the message and appeal of the sacred Scriptures. It

comes in the conviction visited on us by the Holy
Spirit. It comes in the person of Jesus Christ, God's
Son, the living Word of God.

The Word of God is powerful

Now, about God's power. In this nuclear age in
which we live, we have come to think of nuclear
weapons when we think of ultimate power. Years
ago, we used the word nucleus all the time. A nucleus was the center. We never dreamed the word
nuclear would take on so fearful a connotation as it
now possesses.

Christian believers, of all people, should have a
sensible view of the "nuclear threat." What is it that
attracts neutrons so irrevocably to the nucleus of an
atom? My answer: the living breath of God speaking in His world. It is Jesus, the eternal Son, the
express image of God's person, sustaining all
things by His powerful Word (Hebrews 1:3). "In
him all things hold together" (Colossians 1:17).

Few liberals or modernists will agree with me in
that view. They dispute God's sovereignty and His
power. *But they are scared.* Given the world we live
in, the most assuring viewpoint a person can hold
is the one I hold. The voice of God fills His world,
and Jesus Christ, the living Word, holds everything
together.

God's Word speaks to human life — this life so ob-
viously mortal. God's Word speaks to human conscience — a conscience that is only too aware of sin.
God's Word speaks to human sin, exposing its hei-
nous, offensive nature.

Here may be a helpful thought for you. The Word
of God is tuned to speak to man's inner conscience,

but it does not accuse. It does not make charges against a person. Rather, it demonstrates. And it convicts. There is a difference between accusing and convicting.

In court, when an alleged offender stands before the judge, there is a specific charge of violation, there is an accuser and there is evidence intended to back up the charge. Only if the judge is convinced by the evidence and argument will he or she pronounce the alleged offender guilty.

The conviction of the Word of God is different. The Word of God does not single out John Jones or Mary Smith. It does not face up to one or the other and say, "You are a sinner." Instead, it asserts that all have sinned. John Jones or Mary Smith or any other man or woman will know that he or she is a sinner by the living voice of God.

Go to God's Word and you will find that sin is the most pressing, the most compelling, the most imperative problem in human life and society. The most pressing problem is not sickness. It is not war. It is not poverty. *Sin* is the basic problem because sin has to do with a person's soul. Sin does not relate merely to a person's short years on this earth. It involves that person's eternal future and the world to come.

No one has ever overstated the seriousness of the sin question. It is a question that continues age after age. It comes to every human being: "What am I going to do about sin?" That question takes precedence over all other questions that we are called upon to answer. Whether we are world famous or an unnamed member of the human race, we must make confession concerning our relationship with sin.

If each of us is willing to be honest, we will answer, "I have been involved in sin. I have played along with it. I have taken it to my bosom and it has stung me. The virus of sin has entered my lifestream. It has conditioned my mind; it has affected my judgment. I confess I have been a deliberate collaborator with sin."

But sin is more than a disease. It is a deformity of the spirit, an abnormality in that part of human nature which is most like God's. And sin is a capital crime as well. It is treason against the great God Almighty who made the heavens and the earth. Sin is a crime against the moral order of the universe. Each time a man or woman strikes against God's moral nature and kingdom, he or she acts against the moral government of the entire universe.

How does the balance sheet look?

Sinners are always trying to add things up to see how far they must go to deal with the sin problem in their lives. But their moral conscience, if they would honestly listen to it, informs them that only some great resource of merit outside themselves can ever satisfy the obligation. They are head-over-heels in moral debt to the God who made heaven and earth. Every human has a few things he or she thinks are good enough to be put into the necessary fund of merit, but they are never sufficient to pay the debt.

One word describes the sinner. He or she is a rebel, not just in rebellion against his or her own kind, but against God and His kingdom. Suppose a rebellious criminal, locked in one of London's prisons, should ask for an audience with the queen. Such a person, who had struck at the safety of all the queen symbolizes, would have to be pardoned before any other arrangements were even contemplated. He would have to change his lifestyle, for a rebel could not enter the presence of the queen.

But something else would be necessary. He would have to exchange his prison garb for proper dress. Only if he were clean and groomed for the occasion could he expect to be presented to the queen.

That illustration, however imperfect, is a picture of the sinner's plight. If he or she is to stand in fellowship before a holy God, the rebellion must end, there must be forgiveness and pardon, there must be cleansing and the new garments of righteousness. The blood of Jesus Christ was shed for this very purpose. The eternal Son of God has accomplished all this, the just dying for the unjust — an awesome and amazing act by the One who made the worlds and upholds all things by the word of His power.

The writer of the letter to the Hebrews attests that the Son, "after he had provided purification for sins, . . . sat down at the right hand of the Majesty in heaven" (1:3). This is the basic, vital message of Christianity. This is the witness the Christian church, if it is faithful to the revelation God has given it, is proclaiming to the world. Christ Jesus came into the world for the humiliation of death.

He came to deal with the sin question as only God could deal with it.

In the Bible we have the ample record of that day, in the fullness of time, when our Lord Jesus Christ hung between heaven and earth on Calvary's cross. The willing Lamb of God, who had come to bear away the sins of the world, was fulfilling His mission. No one on earth could assist him. In those excruciating hours, after evil men had nailed Him to the cross, the Father in heaven pulled down the blinds; darkness prevailed. It was the eternal Son dying to purge our sins. Alone He suffered. Alone He died. But in that suffering and death He accomplished the sacrifice that has perpetual efficacy.

A once-for-all sacrifice

I need to say something here about the wide difference of viewpoint in Christendom concerning the full meaning of Jesus' sacrifice. Protestant teaching has always been unequivocal: the death of Christ was one finished sacrifice with perpetual efficacy, never to be repeated. But I have read the writings of other theologians who describe dramatically how the Savior dies over and over each time the Mass is said, each time the sacrament is offered. One group insists the sacrificial death of Christ happened once with perpetual efficacy. The other teaches it to be a perpetual, oft-repeated act.

If your Christ must die every Sunday (or Saturday), then you must conclude that His sacrifice was effective for only a week. But if Jesus Christ performed one efficacious act, alone, by Himself, then that act is good for all time and eternity. Admittedly, there is a vital difference between these two viewpoints.

What do the Scriptures teach? They teach that "Christ died for sins once for all, the righteous for the unrighteous, to bring [us] to God" (1 Peter 3:18). Done once, that efficacious sacrifice can never be repeated.

The death and resurrection of Christ has settled the sin question. In believing the good news, we are now forgiven and cleansed—purified from our sins.

There is more good news

But our forgiveness and cleansing by the once-for-all sacrifice of Jesus Christ is only part of the good news. Jesus died, but He rose from the dead. And after His resurrection, He ascended to be seated at the right hand of the Majesty in heaven. In an era of declining morality and open rebellion against God and against His Anointed One, we can take great comfort in this revelation that a majestic, overruling Presence resides in glory.

The Majesty still fills the throne room of heaven. The angels and archangels and seraphim and cherubim continue their celestial praise of "Holy, holy, holy, Lord God Almighty." This is not some far-out concept of some fringe cult. This is straight from the Word of God: When Jesus "had provided purification for sins, he sat down at the right hand of the Majesty in heaven." Jesus returned to the position He had occupied throughout the long, long ages past.

An earnest Christian worker and serious student of the Bible, with whom I have had correspondence, laments the fact that our Christian preaching and teaching does not more clearly identify the risen, ascended Jesus as a *Man*. He has questioned preachers and Christian teachers, many of them well known, "Do you believe that Jesus Christ, now at God's right hand, is a man, or some other being?" Very few of these Christian leaders purportedly believe that Jesus is now a glorified Man. They believe Jesus was a man while He was here on earth, but they tend to believe that He is a spirit now.

After Jesus' resurrection from the dead, He appeared to His disciples. He invited Thomas to feel the wound marks in His flesh. What blessed meaning there is in His words to the fearful disciples: "'Look at my hands and my feet. It is I myself! Touch me and see; a ghost does not have flesh and bones, as you see I have'" (Luke 24:39). Whether modern men and women agree on the exaltation of the Man Christ Jesus, we in the family of God have heard His words and we know the New Testament witness: "'God has raised this Jesus to life, and we are all witnesses of the fact. Exalted to the right hand of God, he has received from the Father the promised Holy Spirit and has poured out what you now see and hear'" (Acts 2:32–33).

The apostle Paul told Timothy, "There is one God and one mediator between God and men, the man Christ Jesus, who gave himself as a ransom for all men" (1 Timothy 2:5). This should be counted as a great victory for Christian believers in our day. Jesus is a Man and He is enthroned at God's right hand. That is significant!

We are joined to Jesus

Jesus is not said to be the victorious God—God is always victorious. How could the sovereign God be anything but victorious? Rather, we take our position with those earliest Christian believers who saw in Jesus a *Man* in the heavenlies. He is a victorious man, and if we are in Him, we too can be victorious.

Through the new birth, the miracle of regeneration, we have been brought by faith into the kingdom of God. As Christians we should recognize that our nature has been joined to God's nature in the mystery of the incarnation. Jesus has done everything He can to make His unbelieving people see that we have the same place in the heart of God that He Himself has. He does so not because we are worthy of it, but because He is worthy and He is the Head of the church. He is the representative Man before God, representing us.

Jesus is the Model Man after which we are patterned in our Christian faith and fellowship. That is why He will not let us alone. He is determined that we will have eyes to see more than this world around us. He is determined that we will have eyes of faith to see God in the kingdom of heaven, and Himself—our Man in glory—seated there in victorious control!

Jesus, Keeper of God's Promises

IS THERE ANYONE AMONG US, any human being, who has not experienced the sadness and disappointment of a promise not kept? More than a few times we have heard an apology, an excuse, perhaps a downright fabrication: "I'm sorry. I thought I could do what I promised you, but I find it is not humanly possible."

That is the language and the experience of human beings. Quite the opposite is our experience when we relate with God. All of God's promises are sure. They are as reliable as His character. Here is how the writer of the letter to the Hebrews puts it:

> When God made his promise to Abraham, since there was no one greater for him to swear by, he swore by himself, saying, "I will surely bless you and give you many descendants." And so after waiting patiently, Abraham received what was promised. (Hebrews 6:13–15)

I must confess that in my ministry I keep repeating some of the things I know about God and His faithful promises. Why do I insist that all Christians should know for themselves the kind of God they love and serve? It is because all the promises of God rest completely upon His character.

Why do I insist that all Christians should search the Scriptures and learn as much as they can about this God who is dealing with them? It is because their faith will only spring up naturally and joyfully as they find that our God is trustworthy and fully able to perform every promise He has made.

God is unchanging

This word concerning God's total faithfulness is a vibrant, positive message in the Hebrews letter. Those to whom it was primarily written were being persecuted. They were suffering. The enemy of their souls was busy planting doubts about God's plans for them and God's promises to them. Probably Satan was sowing doubts about the very character of God who had revealed Himself in a new covenant of grace, sealed in the blood of Jesus, the Lamb of God.

Let me share a conclusion I have come to in my study of the Scriptures. I have come to believe that all the promises of God have been made to assure us weak and changeable humans of God's never-ending good will and concern. What God is today He will be tomorrow. And all that God does will always be in accord with all that God is!

Our Lord will never have to send a message to us, saying, "I am not feeling well today; therefore, I shall not be dealing with you today on the same basis as I dealt with you yesterday."

You may not be feeling well physically today. Have you learned to be thankful anyhow and to

rejoice in the promises of God? God's eternal blessings do not depend on how you feel today. If my
eternal hope rested on how I felt physically, I might
as well begin packing for a move to some other
region! Even if I do not *feel* heavenly, my feelings in
no way change my heavenly hope and prospect.

I dare not relate even a fraction of my faith and
hope to my emotions of the moment and to how I
feel today. My eternal hope depends on *God's* well-
being—on whether God Himself is able to make
good on His promises. And about that there is no
doubt.

God does not play on our emotions

Now that I have brought up the subject of our
human emotions, I should add this further word. I
do not know how familiar you are with the ways of
God and the tender movings of His Spirit. But I
will tell you this quite frankly: God does not play
on our emotions to bring us to the point of spiritual
decision.

God's Word, which is God's truth, and God's
Spirit unite to arouse our highest emotions. Because He is God and worthy of our praise, we will
find the ability to praise Him and to glorify Him.
Some religious and evangelistic techniques are
directed almost entirely to the emotions of those
who are listening to the appeal. They are psychology, not Spirit-directed conviction. They are unre-
lated to the sweet, tender ways of the God of all
mercy and all grace.

I have to disagree with religious appeal that sup-
poses if someone in the audience can be moved to
shed a tear, a saint has been made. Or that if a

husky listener can be touched emotionally to the point that he must blow his nose as though it was Gabriel's trumpet, all will be well with his soul.

I warn you that there is no connection whatsoever between the human manipulation of our emotions, on the one hand, and, on the other, the confirmation of God's revealed truth in our beings through the ministry of His Holy Spirit. When in our Christian experience our emotions are raised, it must be the result of what God's truth is doing for us. If that is not so, it is not properly religious stirring at all.

Jesus has supreme authority

Throughout this letter, the writer leaves us in no doubt concerning the supreme authority vested in Jesus Christ, the eternal Son. Early on, he states the thesis of the letter: Because the message concerning Jesus Christ is true, we must give it our full and complete commitment.

The Holy Scriptures are like that. The Bible is frank, logical, honest. Certain things are true, the Bible is saying, and here they are. And because those things are true, these are your obligations. That is the way God has seen fit to work in His communication with the men and women of this planet.

In the past, there have been those who have looked at what the Bible has to say, and they have reasoned like this: "No argument. Christ carries the supreme authority of God. That leaves us no room to be concerned, no reason to be disturbed. Everything is in God's hands!"

But God's Word declares that it is not quite that

simple. God has made every one of us with a free will. He has made us capable of choosing or rejecting. For us to ignore the authority that God has given to His Son is a grave offense, indeed.

Because of His love for us, God already has taken the initiative. He has left us without room for human excuse. If God cannot get us concerned about His own things and our shortcomings, He cannot do anything at all for us. If His grace and mercy cannot move us, He cannot save us.

This brings us right back to our starting point. Our Christian hope and the promises of God all rest upon the very character of the triune God. We are New Testament believers. We are saved through the terms of a new covenant. That new covenant is based in the love and grace of the One who created us and then gave His life for our redemption.

Of His own free will God has made a pledge and given us a covenant. A Christian is a Christian and remains a Christian because of the bond between the persons of the Godhead and himself or herself.

Psalm 89 states the theme

Note this theme in Psalm 89. In that psalm, the Holy Spirit has dictated a plain message. He goes far beyond the reference to King David. Rather, he is describing David's greater Son, even Jesus, the eternal Son and Lord of all.

The reference is to the kind of covenant a faithful God has made with the people of His choice. The statements made by God to David's progeny and David's people are almost unconditional. God does not make unconditional promises to our race, but these in Psalm 89 are as nearly unconditional as any we will ever find.

The Holy Spirit is not speaking concerning the earthly David who would die. He is speaking of a Son, of whom He says:

> He will call out to me, "You are my Father,
>   My God, the Rock my Savior."
> I will also appoint him my firstborn,
>   the most exalted of the kings of the earth.
> I will maintain my love to him forever,
>   and my covenant with him will never fail.

This Son could be none other than Jesus. And the unfailing covenant God makes with Him is ours. It will never fail because it is God who has promised, and God can be counted on.

I hope what I have been reviewing here is plain. A promise—any promise—is nothing in and of itself. The value of the promise depends on the character of the one who makes it. We know only too well the history of men and women. They make promises and covenants, but often those promises and covenants are broken. They are not kept.

Why covenants fail

There are a number of reasons why human covenants are not kept. Sometimes the person making the covenant has no intention of keeping it. It fails because of the duplicity of the one who promised. In other cases, covenants fail through ignorance. A person makes a promise upon the basis of his or her prospects. But things go badly—physically, financially, intellectually. He or she is unable to fulfill the obligation.

In still other instances, covenants fail because human beings are changeable. A man promises but later changes his mind. He refuses to live up to the terms of the covenant he made. Covenants sometimes fail because the ones who made the promises die. Human mortality causes covenants to become void.

Men and women are well aware of their failures and frailty. They know their weaknesses, their duplicity, their tendency to be less than honest. So they add an oath to their covenant—an appeal to Someone greater than themselves: "So help me, God!"

I have always considered it a little humorous that sinful men who cannot trust each other call on God or the Holy Bible to witness that a sinful being is not going to tell a lie. I suspect there is a chuckle in hell whenever a person in one of our courts promises before God that he or she will "tell the truth, the whole truth and nothing but the truth."

With all of that by way of background, let me tell you my theory. I believe God made an accommodation and went along with our way of doing things. When during Abraham's time He made a promise to save His people, God took an oath to confirm the covenant. And because He could call on no one greater, He swore by Himself! Our faithful God has so sworn for all who will be heirs of the promise.

Shall we not trust Him?

Are we going to trust God? Are we going to commit our entire future to Him? What more assurance do we need than the character of God Himself? It is God's own eternal Person and His faithful character that tell us our salvation is secured through the blood of Jesus Christ, our Savior. It is because God is who He is that we can trust Him and be assured that His covenant will never change.

How rewarding it is to be able to make a proclamation like this! Our forgiveness, our hope for salvation, our confidence in the life to come rest upon God's unchanging love and faithfulness.

I must confess in behalf of all of us that we humans are not as wise as God is. For example, there are men and women forever wishing they might find someone able to predict the future for them. No one can do so with accuracy. Also, we frequently fail to live up to our promises.

But there is no such failure with God. He knows everything that can be known. He is perfect in wisdom. God never has to excuse Himself with a "Well, my intentions were good, but I failed." His ability to deliver on His promises is tied directly to His omnipotence. If God was not omnipotent, He would be unable to keep His promises. He could not give any of us assurance of salvation.

This attribute of God we call omnipotence does not really mean that God can do anything. It means that He is the only Being who can do anything He wills to do. We understand up to a point that God is perfect in love and wisdom, in holiness and strength. Still, it is impossible for us to comprehend what the Lord God means when He says, "I am the holy God." We may, however, come to the understanding that "holy" is the way God is, and that He has made holiness the moral condition necessary to the health of His entire universe.

Because holiness is God's being, He cannot lie.

Because He is God, He cannot violate the holy nature of His being. God does not will to lie. He does not will to cheat. He does not will to deceive. He does not will to be false to His own dear people.

Or to put it positively, in the very perfection of His character, God wills to be true to His children. Because He is perfect and because He is holy, His believing children are safe. Confidently knowing that the Lord God omnipotent reigns, and knowing that He is able to do all that He wills to do, I have no more doubts. I am safely held in the arms of the all-powerful God.

There is no better way to conclude a discussion like this than in the definition of this omnipotent God given in Hebrews:

> Because God wanted to make the unchanging nature of his purpose very clear to the heirs of what was promised, he confirmed it with an oath. God did this so that, by two unchangeable things in which it is impossible for God to lie, we who have fled to take hold of the hope offered to us may be greatly encouraged. We have this hope as an anchor for the soul, firm and secure. It enters the inner sanctuary behind the curtain, where Jesus, who went before us, has entered on our behalf. He has become a high priest forever, in the order of Melchizedek. (Hebrews 7:17–20)

We are in the midst of the storm of life. The believing saints of God are on board the ship. Someone looks to the horizon and warns, "We are directly in the path of the typhoon! We are as good as dead. We will surely be dashed to pieces on the rocks!"

But calmly someone else advises, "Look down, look down! We have an anchor!" We look, but the depth is too great. We cannot see the anchor. But the anchor is there. It grips the immovable rock and holds fast. Thus the ship outrides the storm.

The Holy Spirit has assured us that we have an Anchor, steadfast and sure, that keeps the soul. Jesus — Savior, Redeemer and our great High Priest — is that Anchor. He is the One who has gone before us. He has already entered into the calm and quiet harbor, the inner sanctuary behind the curtain.

Where Jesus is now, there we will be — forever. The Spirit is saying to us, "Keep on believing. Pursue holiness. Show diligence and hold full assurance of faith to the very end. Follow those who through faith and patience inherit what has been promised.

"He is faithful!"

Jesus, Like unto Melchizedek

IT WAS NEVER IN THE MIND of God that a privileged priesthood of sinful, imperfect men would attempt, following the death and triumphant resurrection of our Lord Jesus Christ, to repair the veil and continue their office of mediation between God and man. The letter to the Hebrews makes that fact very plain. When Jesus rose from the dead, the Levitical priesthood, which had served Israel under the Old Covenant, became redundant.

God's better plan for an eternal High Priest and a sinless Mediator is also made plain in the letter to the Hebrews. Jesus glorified at the right hand of the Majesty in the heavens is now our High Priest forever. His priesthood is not after the order of Aaron and Levi but after the enduring priesthood of Melchizedek.

Those are highlights in the Hebrews message concerning the better covenant, the better priesthood and the better hope resting upon the completed work of Jesus Christ for lost mankind. We read:

> Jesus . . . has become a high priest forever, in the order of Melchizedek. . . . When there is a

change of the priesthood, there must also be a change of the law. . . . The former regulation is set aside because it was weak and useless (for the law made nothing perfect), and a better hope is introduced, by which we draw near to God. . . . If there had been nothing wrong with that first covenant, no place would have been sought for another. (Hebrews 6:20; 7:12, 18–19; 8:7)

The mysterious Melchizedek

Long before the time of Moses and Aaron and the sons of Levi, the Genesis record notes the appearance of a mysterious yet compelling personality, Melchizedek. Melchizedek was king of Salem and priest of the most high God. When Abraham returned from the rescue of Lot, his nephew, he was greeted and blessed by Melchizedek. And Abraham gave to Mechizedek the tithe of all the goods he had recovered (Genesis 14:17–20).

The Genesis appearance of Melchizedek is brief and without explanation in Old Testament history. More information is offered by the writer to the Hebrews. When he notes that Melchizedek was "without father or mother, without genealogy, without beginning of days or end of life" (Hebrews 7:3), the writer simply was saying that Melchizedek had no "family tree," no genealogical records through which his origins could be traced. In short, we do not know where he came from.

Melchizedek is not mentioned again until Psalm 110. There he is referred to as the type of an eternal priest of God who would yet appear in Israel's national development.

Jews were very meticulous about genealogy. Each son or daughter of Israel could trace his or her ancestry back to Abraham. It is only too apparent that later generations in Israel did not know how to deal with the references to Melchizedek, a priest whose lineage they could not trace.

The reason all Jews so jealously guarded their lineage, preserving these on permanent tablets, was related to their hope of Messiah's coming. They knew the prophecies. When Messiah finally appeared, He would have to prove His line of descent from Abraham through King David and on down to His own parents.

In his New Testament Gospel, Matthew conformed to Jewish custom, taking pains to furnish his readers a full record of the genealogy of Jesus Christ. He begins with Abraham, Isaac and Jacob, carries the lineage through David and Solomon to another Jacob, concluding with "Joseph, the husband of Mary, of whom was born Jesus, who is called Christ" (Matthew 1:16).

Israel's final hope

In view of the importance given to the Jewish records of ancestry, it is significant that all those carefully preserved records were lost in the Roman destruction of Jerusalem in A.D. 70. So historians believe. Jesus had come as Redeemer and Messiah. Israel rejected Him, crucifying Him on the cross. But there could be no other. No other could have furnished the necessary proof of his descent from Abraham and David. Jesus, the risen, ascended Son of God was and is Israel's final hope.

As we come into a consideration of the things

taught in this section of Hebrews, we must be prepared to do some thinking. We live in a generation that wants everything condensed and predigested. But here we must do some thinking. And in the end, the understanding we achieve will be well worth the effort.

In this part of his letter, the writer sets out to make three things very plain to the troubled Hebrew Christians of his day. First, he declares that the Mosaic law and the Levitical priesthood were not established by God as permanent and perfect institutions. Second, he makes it plain that the eternal and sinless Son came to assure believers concerning His superior and enduring priesthood, confirmed by His glorification at God's right hand. Third, he wants his readers to know that the plan of salvation for sinful men and women does not rest upon earthly offerings made by Levitical priests, but upon the eternal sacrifice and high priestly mediation of Jesus, the eternal Son, who also was willing to become the sacrificial Lamb of God.

The comparisons made in this letter indicate that the provisions of the Old Testament Mosaic law and the system of the Levitical priesthood were interdependent. Thus, when the priesthood was eliminated, the Mosaic law passed away also. The writer's summary is clear: "The former regulation is set aside because it was weak and useless (for the law made nothing perfect), and a better hope is introduced, by which we draw near to God."

We are free in Christ Jesus

What does all this mean to us in our Christian

lives, our Christian faith? Thankfully, it means that we do not stand under the shadow of those laws given through Moses. We do not stand under the shadow of the imperfections of the Old Testament Jewish priesthood and mediation. Instead, we stand in the light and authority of Jesus Christ. He is superior to all Old Testament priests. He has fulfilled the Law—dismissed it, if you will—by the institution of the new covenant based on a superior sacrifice.

This new covenant, sealed in the blood of Jesus, our Savior and Mediator, introduces for us a great spiritual freedom. We should rejoice daily. No one can lay the burden of the old law upon us—a law that Israel was unable to fulfill.

In his letter to the church in Galatia, Paul dealt with this very problem. He states the principle of God's grace and righteousness through faith with telling effect. He condemns those who followed the Galatian Christians around, trying to make Jews out of them. "Stand firm, then," he says, "and do not let yourselves be burdened again by a yoke of slavery. . . . You who are trying to be justified by law have been alienated from Christ; you have fallen away from grace" (Galatians 5:1, 4).

We who are Christian believers should thank God continually for our New Testament guarantees of spiritual life and freedom in Christ! Our sacrifice is not an animal offered by a priest as imperfect as we are. Our sacrifice is the very Lamb of God, who was able and willing to offer Himself to take away the sins of the world. Our altar is not the altar in old Jerusalem. Our altar is Calvary, where Jesus offered Himself without spot to God through the eternal Spirit. Our Holy of Holies is not that section of a temple made with hands, secluded behind a protective veil. Our Holy of Holies is in heaven, where the exalted Jesus sits at the right hand of the Majesty on high.

Note the comparisons

Note the comparison of the two priesthoods. In the Old Testament, every priest who ever served knew that he would ultimately be retired and die. Each priest was temporal. But in our Lord Jesus Christ we have an eternal High Priest. He has explored and conquered death. He will not die again. He will continue as a priest forever, and He will never change! It is for that very reason, the writer assures us, that Jesus is "able to save completely those who come to God through him, because he always lives to intercede for them" (Hebrews 7:25).

Before we move on from the subject of the passing of the Old Testament priestly mediation, I want to mention the strange, anomalous event that took place within the Jerusalem Temple as Jesus gave up His life on the cross. As He "gave up his spirit" (John 19:30) outside Jerusalem, the very finger of God Almighty reached into the temple's most holy place, splitting, rending, tearing the heavy hanging veil.

That ancient veil was not just a curtain. It was a special drape—a veil so thick and heavy that it took several men to pull it aside. As Jesus died, the finger of God rent that veil which had housed the earthly presence of the invisible God. Thus, God was indicating the beginning of a new covenant and a new relationship between mankind and

Himself. He was demonstrating the passing of the old order and the transfer of authority, efficacy and mediation to the new order.

The priesthood, the priests, the old covenants, the altars, the sacrifices—all that had been involved in the Old Testament system of law—was done away with. God had eliminated it as useless, powerless, without authority. In its place He instituted a new Sacrifice, the Lamb of God, the eternal Son, Jesus Christ. God instituted as well a new and efficacious altar, this one eternal in the heavens, where Jesus lives to intercede for God's believing children.

The futile repair

When the Temple veil was torn top to bottom, tradition has it that the Levitical priests determined they must repair that long-sacred partition. And they did. They sewed it together as best they could. Not understanding that God had decreed a new order, they took the earthly view by trying to continue the old system of sacrifices.

I hope I will not be accused of anti-Semitism when I cite certain Bible truths indicating that even yet Jews do not really know why they worship. We evangelicals have no sympathy for those who hate the Jews. In our understanding of the Scriptures and God's great plan, we recognize the worth of our Jewish friends. We have a concern for their well being in an unfriendly world.

Moreover, we believe strongly in the future glory of Israel. We believe that when God's Messiah returns, Israel will minister again in faith and worship in her own land. We believe in a day yet coming when a reborn Israel will shine forth. The Word of God's righteousness will go forth from Zion and the Word of God from Jerusalem.

But for the present, the living, beating life of Jewish faith is gone. There is no altar. There is no Shekinah glory and Presence. There is no efficacious sacrifice for sin. There is no mediatorial priest and no Holy of Holies for him to enter on behalf of his people. All is gone—eliminated as useless, powerless, without further authority.

In its place God has instituted and accepted a new sacrifice—the Lamb of God, the eternal Son. He has confirmed a new and efficacious altar, this one eternal in the heavens, where Jesus ever lives to make intercession for God's believing children. He has ordained and accepted a new High Priest, Jesus, the eternal Son, seating Him at His right hand.

Jesus lives eternally

All that I have been saying may seem complex and involved. This much we must understand: Jesus our Lord, God's Christ and our Savior, lives forevermore! As God is timeless and ageless, so also is Jesus Christ.

And Jesus lives to intercede for us! His eternal interest is to be our surety. We sing of it with faith and joy: "Before the throne my Surety stands; / My name is written in His hands." And then we continue with the rest of those stirring words from the vision and heart of Charles Wesley:

> The Father hears Him pray,
>   His dear anointed One;
> He cannot turn away

The presence of His Son.
His Spirit answers to the blood
And tells me I am born of God.

It is Christ's unfailing intercession that makes it possible for us to tell each other that we believe in the security of the saints of God. We believe there is a place of security, not because there was some technicality that John Calvin might have advanced, but because of the high priestly intercession of the eternal One who cannot die. Day and night He offers our names before the Father in heaven. No matter how weak we may be, we are kept because Jesus Christ is our eternal High Priest in the heavens.

How different is our vision of Jesus Christ from that of the ones who put Him to death, saying, "That is the end of him!" Our vision is of a risen, victorious, all-powerful and all-wise High Priest. Quietly, triumphantly He pleads the worth and value of His own life and blood for the preservation and victory of God's believing children.

Just consider, if you will, the gracious implications of God's guarantee. He declares in His Word that Jesus, our Savior and Mediator, "is able to save completely those who come to God through him, because he always lives to intercede for them." The King James translation reads "is able to save to the uttermost. . . ." There have been preachers who changed the preposition *to* and made it *from*. They preached a salvation with emphasis on what the individual sinner is saved *from*.

I heartily disagree with that emphasis!

Our Lord has given an invitation that excludes no

one. "Whoever" is as broad as the human race. I do not believe God is concerned at all about where we have come from. He is concerned with where we are going. The decision we have made to go where we are going—to be with God forever—is what pleases Him and causes the angels to rejoice.

Some Christian workers have made an entire career of dwelling on the negative aspects of the human, sinful life—"from the uttermost." "Let me tell you what a hopeless drunkard I was!" "Attend the services and let me share what it is like to be a helpless drug addict!" "Come and let me relate the awful, tragic time in my past when I was a good-for-nothing wife-beater!"

It is a gracious thing that God does for us in His mercy and love when we are forgiven, regenerated and converted. It is indeed a new birth! God saves us from what we were, whatever it was. But He expects us to spend the rest of our lives praising Him, telling about the wonders of Christ and His salvation. He wants us to spread the good news of the great eternal future He has planned for us. He wants us to tell others of the eternal habitation He is preparing for all who love and obey Him.

A personal testimony

It is fitting that I close this chapter with a word of testimony. I trust it will be helpful.

I came to Christ and was converted when I was 17. My testimony was just as dull as it is possible for a testimony to be. I had never been in jail. I did not use tobacco in any form. I did not know anything about the use of drugs. I had never taken to any kind of strong drink. I had never deserted my wife—I had never been married!

If you have seen me in later life, you might not believe it, but I was a healthy, red-cheeked young man at the time the Lord found me. There were some who considered me good looking. We had neighbors who said, "Aiden is a fine boy!" If I had had to get up and tell people what I was saved *from*, in the eyes of the curious world my testimony would not have been worth two lines of type.

But I was a sinner in the sight of God and I have found Him faithful. What I was saved *to* is much more important than what I was saved *from*. I have had a lifetime of telling and retelling everyone around me of the goodness, kindness, mercy and grace of God. He has saved me to the uttermost. He guarantees an eternity of fellowship and rejoicing with our Lord Jesus Christ and the redeemed family of God.

If you are doubtful or hesitant, I can only say: Do not make the mistake of trying to match your time on earth against the eternity that is your endless future. No matter who you are, all of your past is time; your future is eternity.

On Christ the solid rock you stand. All other ground is sinking sand.

10

Jesus, One Face of One God

A PERSON CANNOT BE A Christian and deny that the living God has revealed Himself to our sinful race as the sovereign Father, the eternal Son and the faithful Spirit. Yet some professing Christians are so selfishly intrigued by their own expressions of "following Jesus" that they seem unaware that their lives are daily dependent on the promised ministration of Father, Son and Holy Spirit.

For such as these—and actually for all of us in the Christian faith—the writer of the letter to the Hebrews has set forth a compelling and revealing truth: "Christ . . . through the eternal Spirit offered himself unblemished to God" (Hebrews 9:14).

Salvation involves the entire Trinity

How do we effectively teach this to our "babes in Christ" who are prone to say, "I like what I know about Jesus. Surely it is not necessary for me to go beyond that." Our best answer, of course, is a simple statement of Christian doctrine: The Bible makes it plain that the redemption of our lost race was effected on our behalf by the eternal Trinity—God the Father, God the Son and God the Holy Spirit.

We cannot overestimate the full significance of that statement in terms of our redemption and God's atoning work.

There likewise is no ground for a thoughtful, thankful believer to deny that his or her salvation was wrought by the same eternal Trinity—Father, Son and Holy Spirit. This is the whole emphasis of Hebrews 9:14. And it is what I want to emphasize, too.

None of us can ever be fully pleasing to God if we are not willing to be well taught in His Word. I want to be sure that we know what being well taught in the Word means. It does not refer to being well taught in religion. Rather, it is being well taught in the basic concepts necessary to the Christian faith.

One of these basic concepts is the insistence that the crowning achievement of New Testament revelation is the implantation within a believer of a force that impels him or her to act righteously. God has promised this as confirmation that He is able to purge the human conscience from dead religious works, freeing the believer to serve the living God in joy and victory regardless of his or her circumstances in life.

The writer was not suggesting that these early Hebrew Christians, in a time of crisis, lean on religious forms or depend on religious practices. He stressed their need to grasp what God had done for them in a New Covenant centered in Jesus Christ, Savior and Messiah.

Which is more important?

I am reminded that one old saint was asked, "Which is the more important: reading God's Word or praying?" To which he replied, "Which is more important to a bird: the right wing or the left?" The writer to the Hebrews was telling his readers—and telling us—that Christians must believe *all* there is to be believed. They are to do *all* that the Word commands them to do. Those two wings take the Christian up to God!

I sense a spirit of independence, if not rebellion, in the believer who states, "I am not going to bother with the doctrines and the teachings. I am just going to lean back and enjoy Jesus!" It is the path of least resistance. Although I do not wish to scold anyone at this point, it is where many Christians need proper encouragement and godly example.

God has purposefully given us a mental capacity with wide human boundaries. Beyond that, if we are justified, regenerated believers, He has given us an entirely new spiritual capacity. God wants us to believe, to think, to meditate, to consider His Word. He has promised that the Holy Spirit is waiting to teach us. He has assured us concerning all of our blessings in Jesus Christ.

Hebrews 9:14 informs us that Christ, who is God the Son, through the divine Spirit, offered Himself to God, the heavenly Father. Thus we have in the act of redemption the involvement of the Trinity, the Godhead.

Keep in mind that the persons of the Godhead cannot fulfill their ministries separately. We may think of them separately, but they can never be separated. The early church fathers recognized this wholeness of God's person. They said we must not divide the substance of the Trinity, though we recognize the three persons.

No contradictions

Critics often have declared that the Bible contradicts itself in matters relating to the Trinity. For example, Genesis speaks of God's creating the heavens and the earth. The New Testament declares that the Word—God the Son—created all things. Still other references speak of the Holy Spirit's work in creation.

These are not contradictions. Father, Son and Spirit worked together in the miracles of creation, just as they worked together in the planning and effecting of human redemption. The Father, Son and Holy Spirit are consubstantial—going back to the statement of the early church fathers. They are one in substance and cannot be separated.

When Jesus was to launch His earthly ministry, He went to John at the Jordan River to be baptized. The record speaks of the Trinity's involvement. As Jesus stood on the bank of the river following His baptism, the Holy Spirit descended as a dove upon Him and the voice of God the Father was heard from heaven saying, "'This is my Son, whom I love.'"

Similar references remind us of the Trinity's involvement in the glory of Christ's resurrection. During His ministry, Jesus spoke of His coming death. "'Destroy this temple,'" Jesus said, referring to His body, "'and I will raise it again in three days.'" Jesus also declared that the Father would raise Him up on the third day. We are accustomed to saying that the Father raised Jesus from the dead. But in Romans 1 we read that the Spirit of

God declared Jesus to be the Son of God with power "by his resurrection from the dead."

Throughout the Bible record, we have the ever-recurring instances of the persons of the Godhead, the Trinity, working together in perfect harmony. I rejoice in the scriptural assurances of the ministries of the holy Trinity. But I know there are many who confess to problems with the concept of and the teaching concerning the Trinity. If we are going to grasp and appreciate this truth, it will mean diligence on our part. We may need to "pull the weeds" in order that the truth will have soil in which to mature.

Probably we all have wondered at some time or another why our gardens do not produce red tomatoes and yellow corn and green beans without great care and cultivation on our part. Left to themselves, our garden plots will bring forth their own crops of weeds, thistles and briars. This they will do without any help from anyone.

Why? Because the world has been upside down since Adam's fall. God had to say to Adam,

"Cursed is the ground because of you;
     through painful toil you will eat of it
     all the days of your life.
It will produce thorns and thistles for you, . . .
By the sweat of your brow
     you will eat your food. . . ." (Genesis 3:17–18)

A self-demonstrating truth

We are grateful to God for the historical insights of Genesis 3. Adam and Eve fell from their first holy and lofty estate, sinning by transgressing the

Word of their God. That is a statement of fact. But even without the inspired record, we know that the progeny of those first parents are sinners. It is a self-demonstrating truth. The news in our morning paper is proof enough. Hatred is everywhere. Greed surrounds us. Pride and arrogance and violence rule our race. The issue is murder, war and a long list of continuing offenses against one another and against God.

The Scriptures tell us the whole story. Not only have we sinned, but our moral revolt has alienated us from God.

Some people still like to protest God's right to banish the transgressor from His presence forever. They insist upon forming and holding their own humanistic views of God. For that reason I say, let's clear away some of these weeds!

First, there is the old idea that Jesus Christ, the Son, differs from God the Father. People conceive Christ to be a loving Jesus on our side while an angry Father God is against us. Never, never in all of history has there been any truth in that notion. Christ, being God, is for us. The Father, being God, is for us. The Holy Spirit, being God, is for us! That is one of the greatest thoughts we can ever hope to think. That is why the Son came to die for us. That is why the risen Son, our great High Priest, is at the right hand of the Majesty on high, praying for us.

Christ is our advocate above. The Holy Spirit dwelling in our hearts is the advocate within. There is no disagreement between Father, Son and Spirit about the church, the body of Christ.

I must confess that after I became a believer it took some time for me to overcome the feeling that the New Testament was a book of love and the Old Testament a book of judgment. I have given the proposition much time and study, and I am able to make a report. You should know that there are three mentions of mercy in the Old Testament for every one found in the New Testament!

I find there is equally as much recorded in the Old Testament about God's grace and faithfulness as there is in the New. Go clear back to Noah and you will find the record plain: "Noah found favor in the eyes of the Lord" (Genesis 6:8). Favor, or grace, is an Old Testament quality. "The Lord is compassionate and gracious, / slow to anger, abounding in love" (Psalm 103:8).

On the other hand, judgment is a New Testament quality. Read the words of Jesus in the Gospels. Read Peter's warnings. Read the letter of Jude. Read the Revelation. In the New Testament we learn of the terrible judgments God intends to bring upon the world.

God does not change

Why do I mention these things? Because God is a God of judgment, but He is also the God of all grace. God is always the same. He will never change or falter. And when I say *God* I refer to the Trinity—Father, Son and Holy Spirit.

I suspect that many preachers and evangelist have left the false impression in our churches that Christ won God over to our side by dying for us. We have been encouraged to think of the Father as the angry God standing with the club of vengeance, about to destroy sinning mankind. But suddenly Jesus rushes in and takes the blow, allowing us to escape.

That may be good drama, but it is poor theology!

Here is the truth of the matter. The Father in heaven so loved the world that He gave His only begotten Son. It was the love of the Father that sent the Son into our world to die for mankind. The Father and Son and Spirit were in perfect agreement that the eternal Son should die for the sins of the world. We are not wrong to believe—and proclaim—that while Mary's Son, Jesus, died alone, terribly alone, on that cross, the loving heart of God the Father was as deeply pained with suffering as was the heart of the holy, dying Son.

We must ask our Lord to help us comprehend what it meant to the Trinity for the Son to die alone on the cross. When the holy Father had to turn His back on the dying Son by the necessity of divine justice, I believe the pain for the Father was as great as the suffering of the Savior as He bore our sins in His body. When the soldier drove that Roman spear into the side of Jesus, I believe it was felt in heaven.

There is another misconception that has been taught through the years. We have been taught that only one person of the Trinity took part in the plan of redemption. But Hebrews 9:14 tells us that Father, Son and Holy Spirit all had a part. The Father received the offering of the Son through the Holy Spirit.

And what was the offering? It was the blameless and sinless Son, offered as the Lamb of God, without spot and without blemish. The redemptive

JESUS, ONE FACE OF ONE GOD *111*

price was paid by the Son to the Father through the Spirit.

The personal application

There has to be a personal application of these truths. Redemption has flowed down to mankind from the heart of God through His Son by the Spirit. But salvation, to be effective, must be appropriated and confessed. Redemption is an objective thing. It is something outside of us.

Redemption is something that took place on a cross, but salvation is something that takes place and becomes known inside of us! Salvation is redemption appropriated by faith. The three persons of the Godhead continue to call the lost to salvation.

In the Gospels, we read that Jesus ate and talked with sinners. He knew why He was there. He was not approving their wickedness. He was there because it was His nature to offer help and forgiveness and salvation. His critics and enemies saw Him there and asked, "What kind of a religious person are you? How can you eat and talk with sinners?"

Our Lord had an answer. He told them three stories, which are really all one story.

Jesus told them of the 99 sheep in the fold and of the search by the shepherd for the one that was lost. The shepherd would not rest until he had found the lost sheep.

Jesus told them of the woman who treasured a piece of jewelry made up of 10 silver coins. But one of the coins somehow turned up missing, so she got a candle and a broom, and she searched the house everywhere. Suddenly her efforts were rewarded. "I have found it!" she exclaimed with jubilance.

Then Jesus told them of the man who had two sons. The one we would call, in our day, a delinquent. I have never understood why the father gave him his share of the estate when he asked for it. But the father did, and the son set out and soon had squandered all the money. Forsaken by his false friends, he had to feed pigs in their stinking pen to earn something to eat. Finally he said to himself, "What a fool I am! I will return home and be a servant to my father. At least I will have food."

We all know the rest of the story. "I am unworthy!" the boy confessed to his father. But his father forgave him and dressed him in new garments. He threw a great feast and, amid much rejoicing, restored the boy to his place in the family.

The meaning of the three stories

I read and studied those three stories for a long while without being sure I knew what Jesus meant to convey by them. I checked out the commentaries and the reference books; still I was not sure of the meaning. So I sought God alone in earnest prayer to find out what He was trying to say to us as a lost and alienated race. I share with you what the Spirit of God taught me.

Jesus was trying to make plain the searching, seeking, loving ministries of the Trinity – the Godhead. That lost boy was the lost world. That lost sheep was the lost world. That lost piece of silver was the lost world.

The picture that we must see, then, is the Father

looking for the lost son. It is also the Son, the good shepherd, looking for His lost sheep. And it is the Holy Spirit, depicted by the woman with the light, searching for the lost piece of silver. Add them up and you have God's picture of the Godhead working to redeem the human race. Father, Son and Holy Spirit are always seeking the lost treasure.

"*That* is why I eat with sinners," Jesus was saying. "I am the Son, the Shepherd, looking for my lost sheep. My Father is looking for His lost boy. The Holy Spirit is looking for His missing piece of silver."

Father, Son and Holy Spirit are united in their search for the lost. That is our answer for the would-be critics. The Son of God gave the divine offering of Himself, the Holy Spirit conveyed it, and the heavenly Father received it! The Father, the Son and the Holy Spirit—the divine Trinity—were jointly engaged in the great and eternal business of seeking and saving lost men and women.

11

Jesus, Mediator of the New Will

DID YOU KNOW THAT GOD has written a completely new will? And remembered you in it? This will has been in effect ever since the death and resurrection of Jesus Christ. It promises an eternal inheritance through God's unbounded love and faithfulness.

Although it was a transaction that took place two millenniums ago, many people remain unaware that God has included them in His will. The letter to the Hebrews supplies us with the full details. Jesus Christ is Mediator of this new will. His death enabled sinful mankind to be pardoned and to receive an eternal inheritance. Here is what the writer to the Hebrew Christians has to say about it:

> Christ is the mediator of a new covenant, that those who are called may receive the promised eternal inheritance—now that he has died as a ransom to set them free from the sins committed under the first covenant.
>
> In the case of a will, it is necessary to prove the death of the one who made it. . . . In fact, the law requires that nearly everything be

cleansed with blood, and without the shedding of blood there is no forgiveness. . . . Christ did not enter a man-made sanctuary that was only a copy of the true one; he entered heaven itself, now to appear for us in God's presence. Nor did he enter heaven to offer himself again and again, the way the high priest enters the Most Holy Place every year with blood that is not his own. Then Christ would have had to suffer many times since the creation of the world. But now he has appeared once for all at the end of the ages to do away with sin by the sacrifice of himself. Just as man is destined to die once, and after that to face judgment, so Christ was sacrificed once to take away the sins of many people; and he will appear a second time, not to bear sin, but to bring salvation to those who are waiting for him. (Hebrews 9:15–16, 22, 24–28)

This Scripture encompasses so much instruction and so much meaning that we should stand back and view it from a better perspective. It is necessary sometimes to do that with great paintings. We can stand so close to the canvas that we note only the many little details, seeing them out of proportion and perhaps missing entirely the true beauty and meaning of the painting. I suggest we stand back from these verses and gaze in wondering faith as we contemplate God's grand design.

Blood and life are mysteriously related

One thing that I notice immediately is the mysterious relationship between blood and life. God had instructed Israel about this link. "'The life of a creature is in the blood,'" God said, "'and I have given it to you to make atonement for yourselves on the altar; it is the blood that makes atonement for one's life'" (Leviticus 17:11). This instruction concerning blood and the atonement was at the very heart of Israel's religion and her relationship with God. The blood was considered mysterious and sacred. Israelites were never to ingest blood.

The second thing I note is the relationship between sin and death. As human beings, we do not know all there is to know about death. There are religious groups who claim to believe in the annihilation of the human soul and the end of all existence. (Annihilation means to withdraw something from existence.) In the scriptural account of creation God made something out of nothing. But there is no instance in Scripture where God reverses the process of creation and calls an existing thing back into nothingness. Nor is there the concept of annihilation in nature. It is hard, then, to understand why some people want to introduce annihilation into the kingdom of God.

Matter can be—and regularly is—changed. But matter cannot be annihilated. If I strike a wooden match and let it burn to ashes, I can pinch the remaining ash into a smudge on my fingers, but I have not annihilated the elements that were in that match. They merely changed form. Part of the match went up in smoke. Part of it turned to ash. The part that became gaseous continues to possess invisible form in the atmosphere.

Only a change of residence

The living soul within each of us can never be subject to annihilation. There is only a change of residence at the time of death. The soul will change its location, but it will never cease to be. That is the crux of the Bible teaching on the worth and infinite nature of the God-breathed human soul.

Consider this human situation—one many of us have witnessed at one time or another. A mother lovingly holds a tiny baby in her arms, a baby who is alive, cooing, alert, healthy. Then tragedy! Raging disease strikes down that same baby. The mother holds the infant form in her arms, but she is sobbing in grief. Death has robbed her of the object of her affection.

A brief service of loving memory will follow. In the tiny casket, the lifeless baby looks like a still, white angel.

What has happened?

Annihilation?

No! But there has been a change of form and existence—for the parents, a shocking change. The soul within that baby, the active mind, the intelligence, the cooing and laughter—all appear to have passed away. The lifeless body will be laid tenderly in the earth, where it finally will return to dust. But that living, individual soul will not be annihilated. Never! The soul has changed its place of existence, but it has not ceased to be.

Death has two forms

I am amazed by the number of people who do not seem to know that the Bible speaks of two forms of death. We believe the Bible when it says physical death is the reality facing every person born into the world. But there is also a very evident condition among us described as spiritual death. We trace it back to the Garden of Eden and the warning of God to our first parents: "'You are free to eat from any tree in the garden; but you must not eat from the tree of the knowledge of good and evil, for when you eat of it you will surely die'" (Genesis 2:16–17). Adam and Eve did not heed the warning; they ate of the forbidden fruit. And on the day that they transgressed the law of God in disobedience and self-will, they died spiritually.

Death is not annihilation. Death is not cessation of existence. Death is a changed relationship in a different form of existence.

When Satan, a creation of God, rebelled in pride and disobedience, he was saying, "I will arise and put my throne above the throne of God!" And right there Satan died. But he did not cease to be. God expelled him from heaven and from fellowship with Himself. He cast him down to earth. And after all these centuries, Satan is still around. He was not annihilated, and his eternal judgment is still to come.

Men and women try to ignore the fact of spiritual death. The Scriptures do not. Paul has a classic one-sentence commentary on the subject. He says the woman "who lives for pleasure is dead even while she lives" (1 Timothy 5:6). She was not dead physically, but spiritually she was cut off from God. Her form of existence was such that she was not related to, but separated from, God.

The apostle also warns us that death is one of

sin's fearful consequences. Sin came into the world and brought death with it. The soul that sins will die. So the Bible declares.

Sin ends at death

Another thing we see in the Hebrews Scripture earlier quoted is that God has a very simple way of dealing with sin. God terminates sin in death! I lived in Chicago when the notorious killer gangster, John Dillinger, was being hunted. The police printed pictures of Dillinger with warnings about his violence with guns. Always he was shown with a cynical, sarcastic smile on his face. But the final picture indicated that he had stopped sinning. He was lying on his back, toes up. He was covered with a sheet. Dillinger was dead.

Sin ends at death. When a person dies, he or she will sin no more. That is God's way of ending sin. He lets death terminate it.

God's Word makes it clear that the life touched and tainted with sin is a forfeited life. The soul that sins shall die. The wonder that we will never fully understand is that God wanted to save our forfeited lives. So He allowed the blood of the divine Savior to be offered on our behalf. Notice that there must be a blood atonement because blood and life have a vital, mysterious relationship.

The blood of Jesus Christ is of infinite value. The pouring out of blood indicates the termination of life. Because the blood of Jesus Christ, the eternal Son, the Lamb of God, was poured out, our acts of sin may be pardoned.

We need to give this spiritual truth all the reverence and contemplation it deserves. Do we talk too loosely about the price of our redemption? I confess that I cringe just a little when I hear someone speak about Christ paying our debt—buying us back. Sometimes we make it sound like nothing more than a business deal. But I do not like to think of God redeeming us in the way we might redeem a cow or a horse at some livestock show. In God's plan for redeeming us there is something higher and holier, more sweet and beautiful.

In the Old Testament, the sacrifices and offerings and the poured-out blood of animals were efficacious in ceremonial symbolism. But the death of Jesus Christ was efficacious actually and eternally. (*Efficacious* is a word theologians like to use; it simply means that it works. It is effective. You can count on it.) When Jesus poured out His blood on Calvary, He guaranteed eternal redemption to all who would put their trust in Him.

The blood and the life are one. When the blood was poured out, when Jesus Christ the eternal Son died, His death became vicarious. (*Vicarious* is another word that needs a brief explanation. A vicarious act is one performed on behalf of someone else. When Jesus died at Calvary, it was a vicarious death. Jesus died on behalf of us all, the innocent One for the guilty many.)

The atoning, vicarious death of Jesus Christ for sinful humanity is at the very foundation of the Christian faith. For those who think they can find a better way than God's way, it is not a popular teaching. But there is no other way. Jesus is the *only* way.

If you are a believing, trusting, joyful Christian, never let anyone rob you of this assurance and consolation. Allow no one to edit or change this basic truth—trying to make it more acceptable to philosophy or literature or art or religion. Let this wonderful truth stand tall in its beauty and effectiveness. Christ died, and in the giving of His life, He died vicariously!

God's holiness and justice are satisfied

In Christ's atoning death the holiness and justice of God have been satisfied. God no longer holds anything against us, for we have come to Him in faith. We have pleaded as our merit only the vicarious, efficacious death of our Savior and Lord. And as we have believed, we have found the power of death broken.

The writer of the letter to the Hebrews assures us that Jesus has become the mediator—the executor—of the new covenant, the new testament in God's grace and mercy. The word *mediator* comes from the verb "to mediate." A mediator is one who stands between two parties or two factions needing to be reconciled.

The Bible lets us know how far sinful mankind is from a holy God. Sin has dug a vast separating gulf. Christ has become the Mediator. By the giving of Himself in death, He stands between God and sinners. He shows us that by His death He has made effective God's testament, God's will.

That contract into which God has entered guarantees reconciliation. We are reconciled to God! God's gracious new will—His contract—guarantees pardon. We may be restored into the household of God by faith.

Death made the will effective

Let me share with you another observation simple in concept but profound in this context of our divine inheritance. As long as the Lord Jesus lived, God's new covenant and will for us could not become effective. It became immediately effective the instant Christ died. The death of the Testator brought immediate pardon, forgiveness, cleansing, fellowship and the promise of eternal life. Such is the bountiful and enduring legacy that has come by faith to the believing children of God as a result of Jesus' Calvary death.

I want to conclude by pointing out something that will sound strange to any mortal human being. No man ever died to make his will valid and then came back to earth as the executor of his will. No one. Some other person always acts as executor and administrator of the estate that has been left.

But what no mortal has done, Jesus Christ, the eternal Son of God, has achieved. He has accomplished this kind of enduring administration and divine beneficence. Jesus died to activate the terms of the will to all its beneficiaries; Jesus rose in victory from the grave to administer the will.

Is that not beautiful? Jesus did not turn God's will over to someone else to administer. He Himself became the Administrator. Many times He declared, "I will be back. I will rise again on the third day!" He came back from the dead. He rose on the third day. He lives to carry out for His people all the terms of His will.

We must continue to trust this Living One who is now our great High Priest in the heavens. There is not a single argument in liberal theology strong enough to pry us from our faith. We have a living hope in this world, and that living hope is equally valid for the world to come.

Oh, yes. I should tell you exactly who are named in God's new will.

The answer is Christ's answer and invitation. *Whosoever!* "Whoever wishes, let him take the free gift." Amen.

12

Jesus, Fulfillment of the Shadow

IMAGINE WITH ME a capable housewife and cook preparing her dining room for guests. She has set the cloth-covered table with her best china and silverware, positioning everything precisely. She adds a centerpiece of cut flowers – a delicate floral complement to the food we suppose will soon be coming.

But instead of the platter of savory beef and the dishes of steaming mashed potatoes and other vegetables that we had anticipated, she brings a single loaf of bread into the dining room. This she upends on the buffet, placing a strong light behind it so that the loaf of bread casts its own distinct shadow over the table service beyond it. We would have further reason to question the woman's sanity if at that point she called family and guests to the table, announcing cheerily, "The shadow of the bread is ready. You may come!"

Before I attempt a spiritual application of that unlikely scenario, consider how the writer to the Hebrews portrays the vast difference between the Old Testament "shadow" in the law and the reality of God's glory in the person of Jesus Christ, our Savior and Lord:

> The law is only a shadow of the good things that are coming – not the realities themselves. For this reason it can never, by the same sacrifices repeated endlessly year after year, make perfect those who draw near to worship. If it could, would they not have stopped being offered? . . .
>
> Then he said, "Here I am, I have come to do your will." He sets aside the first to establish the second. And by that will, we have been made holy through the sacrifice of the body of Jesus Christ once for all. . . .
>
> When this priest had offered for all time one sacrifice for sins, he sat down at the right hand of God. (Hebrews 10:1–2, 9–10, 12)

The inspired writer is plainly repetitious in his effort to fully contrast the Old Testament rituals, or shadows, with the perfections of grace, mercy and love found in the radiant, eternal person of Jesus, the Christ. This is a serious, sobering passage of Scripture, for it deals with the hope and the glory of the human race.

Shadow versus reality

The Old Testament economy, the law of Moses, the priesthood of imperfect men and the offering of sacrifices for sin – all of these were appointed of God for a time. They represented as a shadow the better things, the reality to come.

The Old Testament rituals contained the meaningful shadow of the promised Messiah-Redeemer.

The writer is telling us that the true Light of God had fallen across the person of Jesus, the eternal Son. The shadow cast by that light and that Person was the temporary economy of the Old Testament.

We know very well the impossibility of trying to survive on a shadow. It cannot be done. The shadow has been cast by the light, but it has no being or substance of its own. If you are in need of nourishment, the shadow of a loaf of bread is of no avail. It will provide no food. You will continue to be hungry. You will say, "I have had enough of shadow. Bring me the actual loaf of bread so I may eat and be satisfied!"

So in those Old Testament times, the shadow of good things to come was not enough. Men and women with whom God was dealing had to live by looking forward in faith to the better promise, the better hope, the reality to come. This is the glory and joy of the letter to the Hebrews. Jesus has come to be Savior and Messiah and Lord. God's Reality has come! The shadow has been fulfilled. The radiance of God's glory in the person of Jesus Christ has made the shadow of no effect.

When we find repetition in the pages of our Bibles as we do in these early chapters of Hebrews, we know there is a purpose behind it. As Christian believers, we have learned to trust the divine wisdom and the leading of the Holy Spirit of God. The Spirit knows that we do not quickly apprehend divine truth. We must read or hear it more than once. God's method of instruction is "Do and do, do and do, / rule on rule, rule on rule; / a little here, a little there" (Isaiah 28:10) – until we have received and learned and benefited.

In this process of learning, God has some problems with us. One problem is that we get bored. Thankfully, God is faithful and persistent. He is not disposed to let us go. He keeps telling us to go on learning, to go on believing, to go on rejoicing in His Word. He is God and we can trust Him as He leads us and reveals His will to us.

Now, on God's side I speak with reverence but with plainness when I say that God became tired of those Old Testament rituals and sacrifices. It is not possible that the blood of bulls and goats can purge away sin. God says as much through the prophet Isaiah:

> "The multitude of your sacrifices—
>   what are they to me?" says the Lord.
> "I have more than enough of burnt offerings,
>   of rams and the fat of fattened animals;
> I have no pleasure in the blood of bulls and
> lambs and goats.
> When you come to meet with me,
>   who has asked this of you,
>   this trampling of my courts? (Isaiah 1:11–12)

Our hearts must be in tune with God

In effect, Isaiah was saying to the people of Israel, "God grows weary of your sacrifices and offerings when your hearts and minds are not in tune with Him!" Probably if we are sufficiently thoughtful and concerned, this same message would cause us to reassess a popular notion among us. We presume we are impressing high heaven by attending churches in large numbers. Surely God is still asking, "Who told you to do this? When you come before Me, who has required this of you? Bring no more vain oblations!"

God is bored with interminably repeated sacrifices and offerings that have no meaning. He had initiated those rituals and sacrifices in Israel, but only as temporary measures for the covering of sin until the Messiah-Redeemer should come. When Israel no longer had a commitment in worship and no sense of the importance of forgiveness and obedience, God said, "I cannot stand the empty motions you go through. I hate your rituals and feasts. They are a trouble to me. I am weary of them."

Ultimately, there came the word from the eternal Son, repeated in Hebrews 10:5:

> "Sacrifice and offering you did not desire,
>   but a body you prepared for me;
> with burnt offerings and sin offerings
>   you were not pleased.
> Then I said, 'Here I am—it is written about me
>   in the scroll—
> I have come to do your will,
>   O God.'"

This can be none other than Jesus, the eternal Son, the Lamb of God slain from the foundation of the world. He has come to carry out God's gracious plan of redemption. Thus it is that by that will of God "we have been made holy through the sacrifice of the body of Jesus Christ once for all."

What have we done with this message?

Have we really accepted this word from God Himself?

I am of the opinion that much in our Christian

ritual and liturgy does not come to grips with its basic meaning. I have listened to the great musical renditions of Bach, Beethoven, Handel and others. The music written for use in services such as the mass is sublime and the language beautiful. But I cannot escape the feeling that something is missing. The prayers and the appeals are there—"Lord, have mercy!" "Christ, have mercy!" They are voiced again and again.

Could it be that this prayer, this appeal to God for mercy, is but the shadow of the truth? Do these prayers never approach to the reality of saving faith and confident assurance in God's promise and provision? There must come a time when petition becomes reality and we shout, "It is done! The great transaction is done! I am my Lord's, and He is mine!"

There has to be a time and a place when we rejoice in faith that we are forgiven, that we have been born again, that God has accomplished His plan. Right there we drive a stake and say, "Thank you, Lord! I am forgiven. I am cleansed. I am pardoned. I am a new person, born from above. Now put me to work. I am ready to witness."

I confess that I am sad indeed for those multitudes in the great framework of Sunday Christianity who know nothing beyond their plaintive and continuing efforts to be forgiven and to find mercy. They must come to the time when it is done, when they can stretch their hands toward heaven and say in triumphant faith, "It is finished!"

Substance, not shadow

This is the contrast between law and grace. In

Old Testament times, every priest ministered daily, offering the same sacrifices that could not take away sin. Then came the revelation of the new covenant and the eternal, once-for-all sacrifice of Jesus Christ and the assurance of complete forgiveness:

> When this priest had offered for all time one sacrifice for sins, he sat down at the right hand of God. Since that time, he waits for his enemies to be made his footstool, because by one sacrifice he has made perfect forever those who are being made holy. . . .
>
> Therefore, brothers, since we have confidence to enter the Most Holy Place by the blood of Jesus, by a new and living way opened for us through the curtain, that is, his body, and since we have a great priest over the house of God, let us draw near to God with a sincere heart in full assurance of faith. (Hebrews 10:12–14, 19–22)

Where could we find a more gracious picture of the privileges that belong to the believing, trusting children of God? Notice that we have been provided a consecrated way into the very presence of God! What a contrast to the Old Testament picture of our first parents when they had sinned and failed in the Garden of Eden. God had to say to them, "Get up and get out!" As they left that beautiful estate and God's presence, God placed "cherubim and a flaming sword flashing back and forth to guard the way to the tree of life" (Genesis 3:24).

It was the beginning of trials and sorrows for the human race, represented then by Adam and Eve. They could never return. And it has been my feeling that the whole race has harbored a yearning to go back to God's presence, to return to Eden. I do not mean that everyone in the race wants to be a Christian. Too many are satisfied with the world, the flesh and the devil. But when you come to really know men and women, you often will find a wistful yearning, a longing probably not identified, to know what it meant for Adam and Eve to be able to dwell contentedly in the presence of their God and Creator.

In it all we see the blinding effect of sin. Men and women do not really want to be good. They do not want to submit to the will of God. Yet the longing for that Presence still is there.

But no one, unaided, has found a way back. Men and women everywhere have tried. It is said that in India there are enough gods for each person to have his or her own. Where is the tribe or nation without *some* god to worship or appease? But the search for a way back has been an empty disappointment.

And then Jesus came to live among mankind. The inspired record has Him saying, "'I have come to do your will, O God'" (Hebrews 10:7). After His death and resurrection, He opened a new and consecrated way back into the presence of God. He blazed the trail as our divine Mediator. Through faith in Him, all who yearn to may enter again the very presence of God.

And there in that Presence, Jesus is our great High Priest and Mediator. Because He wears our human nature, He welcomes us, His brothers and sisters, to share His position in the heavenlies.

Jesus took our guilt, *but* . . .

In this context we should consider our justification and our acceptance by the living, holy God. In our Christian faith we understand that God laid on Christ the iniquity of us all. Theologians sometimes call this the "transfer of guilt," and I believe what the Bible says about it.

In many church circles today we are hearing about the "automatic" qualities attached to Christianity. A whole generation is being taught that a profession of faith in Christ brings automatic righteousness, automatic standing with God, automatic pardon and automatic eternal life. "Jesus has done everything that needs to be done," goes the argument; "all you have to do is say you believe. Believe and be justified! Believe and be accepted as righteous!"

This idea of automatically transferring the sinner's guilt to Christ is a little too pat to please my heart. The commonly held idea seems to be that I can be as vile as the inside of a green, mucky sewer, but if and when I believe, the Lord drops a mantle of judicial righteousness upon me and immediately I am accepted by God as perfectly pure. It is my conclusion that a holy God would have to contradict Himself to perform a transaction like that.

How does God justify a sinful person? He does so by taking the sinner's nature into Christ, who is the perfect, righteous One. His righteousness, in turn, goes to the sinner. Some teachers will argue for the judicial impartation of righteousness alone. But when by faith the sinner's nature is taken into the very nature of Christ, His righteousness becomes a part of the former sinner's nature.

Let me say it another way. I doubt very much that there is any such thing in the mind of God as justification without regeneration—new God-life imparted to the sinner. It is regeneration that unites us to the nature of Jesus. Jesus being righteous imparts new God-life from His own nature to us, and God is satisfied.

In that sense, the idea of the transfer of guilt is accurate. But we carry the concept too far until it becomes a plainly mechanical thing, like a commercial transaction. There must be a vital, living commitment. Righteousness is imparted to the believing sinner who is united to Christ. It is not imparted to the sinner who simply stands outside and receives a judicial notification that he has been "made righteous."

This adds some important light. As believers, we are accepted *in* the beloved Son. We can never be accepted *out of* the beloved Son.

God is our hiding place

Christian believers have another privilege. We have seen that we have a moral right to come to God—into His presence. We are accepted by Him because of Christ Jesus. But we also have the right to hide in God and be safe. That, too, is our privilege because Jesus, our great High Priest, perfectly represents us at God's right hand. When we are united to Christ, no one can take this right and privilege away from us. We are safe! We are safe!

Someone was quoted as saying, "I do not want to hide from life. I want to face up to life every day."

Knowing the nature of humankind, I would call such talk bold and brave.

When the winter temperature is 50 degrees below zero, it is brave, bold talk to say, "I do not want to hide from the cold. I want to face it, whether I have the proper clothing or not!" When we face the abrasive storms of life, it is ridiculous to say, "I do not want a hiding place. I will face the storms."

What we are hiding from is not life. We are hiding from a sinful world, from a sinister devil, from vicious temptation. We are hiding in the only place there is to hide—in God. It is our right and our privilege to know the perfect safety He has promised.

The trusting child of God is safe in Jesus Christ. When the lambs are safe in the fold, the wolf can growl and snarl outside, but he cannot get into the fold. When the child of God enters the Father's house, the enemy of his or her soul can roar and threaten, but he cannot enter. Such a shelter is our high privilege!

Jesus is enough

In Old Testament terms—the shadow of reality—God promised He would cover the sin of His people. In the New Testament covenant, God declares He will put our sin away forever. This is a vastly different thing! "Christ was sacrificed once to take away the sins of many people; and he will appear a second time, not to bear sin [that is, without a sin offering], but to bring salvation to those who are waiting for him" (Hebrews 9:28).

God chose eight and perhaps nine writers to provide us with the New Testament. These inspired

Scriptures agree that the symbolic shadows in the Old Testament have given way to the new covenant of grace and pardon mediated through Jesus Christ, who died and rose again. We look back with gratitude and love to His atoning death at Calvary. We look forward in hope and expectancy to His second coming.

This all adds up to the fact that Jesus Christ is enough for all our needs. He is our great High Priest and Intercessor in heaven. He is the worthy Lamb of God, slain from the foundation of the world. By His blood He has consecrated forever the way into God's presence. He is our Man in glory.

Let us thankfully hide in Him and be safe!